Self- Amused

Self-➤
Amused

A Tell-Some Memoir

PETER FUNT

Jefferson Bay Books

Published by Jefferson Bay Books.

ISBN: 978-0-578-91662-0

Printed in the United States

First Hardcover Edition: July 2021

Please direct inquiries regarding excerpts from this book, video clips or interviews to: Media@CandidCamera.com.

In loving memory of my mother, Evelyn Funt,
who always believed in me.

I remember in eighth grade proudly bringing home
a composition that had earned me a rare "A."
The next morning, Mom wrote on the back:
"Rice Krispies, peanut butter, 2 cukes, ¾ lb. bologna, Ajax."

CONTENTS

CONTENTS

*Self-Amused people do shit they find funny because they find it funny
and are therefore amused by it. These people find loads of things
amusing, from the little things to the negative things. Their emotions
are not influenced by the negative vibes of others.*
—Urban Dictionary

FOREWORD

FULL DISCLOSURE: This is not the real foreword.

The actual foreword, in which I introduce myself, was moved after it came to my attention that it would not be counted toward the total number of pages. Apparently forewords are marked with letters instead of numbers—what you are reading now is page i, after which (if I were foolish enough to keep writing) would come ii, and iii, and then iv. Actual numbers come into play with Chapter One (which I've decided is Page 15). Just imagine the embarrassment for an author if her book were listed on Amazon as being 76 pages, when in fact it had a 200-page foreword that was never counted. As an author of few words, that's a risk I can't take.

Sorry.

1 / NOT A FOREWORD

FULL DISCLOSURE: This is not my first book.

Many of you, even my fan, might find that puzzling. You're telling yourself, "How odd. I don't recall seeing any of Peter's books before."

That's because, for reasons understood only among publishing professionals, there is a complicated system by which most manuscripts are rejected before folks belonging to a group known as the *general public* can read them. The last time I wrote a book a respected agent emailed:

"I think that because the book is so specific to your experiences it lacks the universality that many memoirs have. As you know, most memoirs these days follow a particular arc: they tell a story of transcendence over troubling and often horrifying circumstances. Obviously, this is not your life!"

She really nailed it! My life has zero universality. However, I have had my share of horrifying circumstances, such as sitting in my son's car at 3 a.m. as it filled with water during a fierce storm and trying for over an hour to stop the horn from blasting. Or twice getting hit in the face with baseballs. Or having blood rush to my head as I hung upside down from a 10-foot ceiling as part of a "Candid Camera" prank. Things like that seemed pretty horrifying at the time.

Another agent said:

"We didn't have a clear vision of the audience to which your book might be pitched." Her rejection noted that what I had written "feels extremely specific in its anecdotes and interests."

Guilty as charged. When I wrote about watching Clint Eastwood cuddle a baby pig, or trying to argue my own case in LA Superior Court, or telling a player on the New York Yankees that he rubbed his crotch too much during games—those were, I'll admit, very specific.

Several agents and editors advised me that my books needed a message, sometimes referred to as a *takeaway*. For instance, when I share a story about pranking Cybill Shepherd by hitting her with a four-tiered birthday cake and finding that she got quite upset about it, readers want advice. Something like: As you go through life, don't hit temperamental Hollywood stars with cake.

I was approached by a guy who earns a ton by writing books for aspiring business people. (Because he has sold X-thousand copies he is frequently referred to as a *guru*.) He said I should write a book for what he called "the business community," and he even had the title figured out: "Candid Clues to Better Business."

"Once we have the book," he explained, "the fee for lectures goes way up." (Note that the project now had a "we" in it.) The book and the speeches would draw from the vast library of "Candid Camera" clips, covering my father's illustrious career as well as my years doing the show.

"What are the clues?" I asked.

"Don't worry. Collect the funniest clips and the insights will be apparent. This book will practically write itself!"

If there's one thing I learned during years of failure it's that books do not write themselves—although Amazon is probably working on it. Still, I gathered the clips: "The Car Without a Motor," "The Sideways Elevator," "The Flight to Nowhere," and a half-dozen others. As I feared, there were no takeaways. The best advice I could come up with for business people: If you're bored doing megadeals, take a relaxing break by watching "Candid Camera" clips on YouTube.

◆ ◆ ◆

WHEN I WAS IN MY TWENTIES I thought getting a book published was so simple even my friend Mike Shatzkin and I could do it. That we succeeded (in getting published, not making money) has haunted me for decades. The project was "Gotcha," a book about how to prank people, which made great sense from a marketing perspective. Here was the son of Allen Funt, TV's best-known trickster, sharing secrets about how to do your own gags. It also made sense from a business perspective because Mike was the son of a top publishing executive and got us a deal with Grosset & Dunlap.

I enjoyed doing research for "Gotcha," learning, for example, that Abe Lincoln was an inveterate prankster (tying a string under a bed in the honeymoon suite at a local hotel, running it through a hole in the floor to the room below and attaching a bell, so Abe and his buddies could howl with laughter each time the bell rang). But as for the how-to elements of the book, I had little to draw upon. Our made-for-TV gags didn't translate to private life, which is to say no one at our house ever sat on a whoopee cushion or drank from a dribble glass. I proceeded to conjure up a few dozen "tried-and-true jokes" that were not true and, to my knowledge, had never been tried.

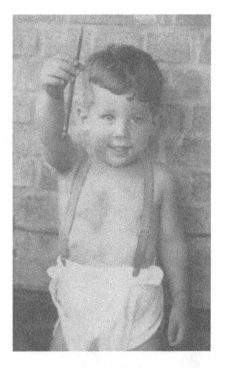

I began writing at age one, but failed to be published for over 20 years.

An example:

Imagine the frustration of starting a car, pulling away from the curb, and immediately hearing a strange rattling sound. When the car stops, the noise stops. All it takes is a handful of nuts and bolts secretly placed in the victim's hubcap. Even better, remove the victim's hubcap and take it home for several hours of preparation. Use the upside down hubcap as a mold into which you pour water, then drop in the nuts and bolts. Place the hubcap in a freezer until the water becomes solid ice. Replace the hubcap. When the victim drives his car the nuts and bolts will gradually be released as the ice melts. The driver travels for several miles before he hears anything, then the rattling noise begins and slowly builds—as if the car is falling apart bit by bit.

I have no idea if what I described would actually work. That was true of all the gags in "Gotcha," which was published as a $7.95 hardcover but never earned back its modest advance. The book did get me a guest appearance on the "Today" show for an April Fools segment, but the joke was on me. I appeared with some guy who had written a college paper about pranking and the host, Maria Shriver, asked him for some history. He spoke for roughly five minutes at which point Shriver apologized for being out of time.

Recently I checked the Amazon site for used copies of "Gotcha" and found this:

Gotcha! by Peter Funt (1980-02-03)

Hardcover

$930^{35}

$3.95 shipping
Only 1 left in stock - order soon.

More Buying Choices
$918.28 (4 used & new offers)

Okay, maybe with inflation $930.35 is a fair price. But $3.95 for shipping? Come on!

I considered online courses that teach you how to write a bestseller, and found one offered by a guy named Mark Dawson titled "How to Write a Bestseller." It costs a mere $297, but I lost interest when I read in Publisher's Marketplace that Dawson weaseled his way onto the *Sunday Times* bestseller list by purchasing 400 copies of his own book.

By far the most annoying advice I got from experts in the book business was that I should consider self-publishing. This used to be known as vanity publishing back in the days when only certified egomaniacs would spend thousands of dollars to have a book professionally printed. Today anyone can upload a manuscript and, for just a few bucks, have it printed and offered on

Amazon where tens of people might buy it.

I'm not keen on self-publishing any more than I am on, say, self-dentistry (full disclosure: I had people try self-dentistry as a "Candid Camera" gag and it was very funny). But after taking stock of my frustrations as an author, I found my takeaway:

Writing a memoir—in fact, most of life—works best if you are easily Self-Amused.

2 / WELL HUNG

AFTER DECADES doing "Candid Camera" I still don't have all the answers, but I have heard most of the questions.

Is it really real? Abso-f-ing-lutely. My father and I based the entire concept—and our reputations—on making "Candid Camera" real. Some competitors, whom I'll discuss later, have faked hidden-camera scenes. Not us. Frankly, much of our material is funny simply because it is spontaneous and unrehearsed.

Have you ever been sued? Ha. Only once, and I'll save that twisted tale for Chapter 18.

How many Emmy awards has "Candid Camera" won? None. No Emmy, Golden Globe or Peabody. We haven't even received a *TV Guide* viewers' honorable mention certificate. We did, however, win one special award. A national plumbing supply company gave us a trophy because our slogan—"Smile, you're on Candid Camera"—was found to be the most popular graffiti above restroom urinals.

Are people harder to fool these days? No! Folks are easier to fool. That may seem counterintuitive, but I'm certain it's true. Much of it has to do with multitasking. When Dad did the show he had to work at distracting people. These days they do it to themselves.

Many people we now encounter are fiddling with personal devices, tackling routine activities with less-than-full focus. That makes them easier targets for our little experiments, but also more vulnerable to mishaps and genuine scams.

In doing recent versions of our show I worried briefly that people are now so tech-savvy that some of our props and fake setups wouldn't be believed. Instead, we found that the omnipresence of technology has reached a point where people will now accept almost anything.

We showed customers at a salon an "un-tanning machine" that ostensibly sucked off dark pigment in seconds. We notified residents in a Denver suburb that they would be getting mail delivery via drone. We told patients at a dentist's office that they'd now be performing a DIY dental exam. In each case, just about everyone bought in. At the dental office, several people were even prepared to give themselves a shot of Novocain before we intervened.

I don't necessarily believe 21st-century Americans are more gullible, but they tend to give that impression by protesting life's little insults without taking time to fully digest the situation.

For instance, we told shoppers in Seaside, Calif., they would be charged a "$10 in-store fee" for not buying online. We told customers at a New York City food store that to pay with a credit card they would need "three forms of photo ID." We hired a cop in Scottsdale, Ariz., to enforce a "2 m.p.h. pedestrian speed limit."

Virtually everyone took these propositions to be true. They shot back quickly at big government, big business or any other entity that seemed to have too big a role in managing their lives.

We tried a few political experiments and the results were predictable. We showed New Yorkers petitions to recall state officials, but the names were all fictitious. Most people supported the effort, among them a lawyer who carefully explained that one should never sign anything without complete knowledge of the facts, and then signed anyway. In California, our actress posing as a candidate obtained dozens of campaign signatures without ever stating a position, a party or even her full name.

In Arizona, we hired two actors to portray "illegal immigrants." One played a well-dressed gentleman from England, the other a blue-collar worker from Mexico. The British fellow got plenty of signatures to "vouch for good character," while the Mexican guy had difficulty just getting people to stop and listen to his plea.

One thing that surprised us is the frequency with which people now whip out phones to record whatever strange situation we create. When we rigged a self-serve yogurt machine to start but never stop, one young customer took video for two full minutes. When we arranged to have a store institute a "gays- only" policy, one startled patron conducted (and recorded) his own interview with our actor—essentially producing the "Candid Camera" show without realizing he was on it.

I don't mind the smartphone obsession in our scenes; it's rather funny. It is a shame, though, that so many people now interrupt real life—in effect hollering "cut"—to record what could be called Act One. In doing so they spoil their own Act Two.

Much hasn't changed for us over the years. For example, I expected to encounter more profanity in everyday conversation, but it's really not there. I also wondered whether young people would be less spontaneous when caught in our scenarios, yet there's no hint of that whatsoever. I thought in these litigious times fewer people would sign a waiver to appear on our show, but the percentages have stayed about the same over the years.

I do note that today more people step out in public looking a bit disheveled and unkempt and are then hesitant to sign because they're not happy with their appearance. Fortunately for our show, people are still, for the most part, willing to engage a stranger and to smile when a little joke is revealed. That said, many folks are feeling the weight of the world's problems, perhaps more than before.

It seems the less able we are to control the macro aspects of our lives, the more we dwell on minutiae. That might explain why strangers stood on a street corner for many minutes to help our actress select the best cell-phone picture of her dog. Folks listened with surprising curiosity as our actor explained why he needed change for a dime.

Posing as a sanitation worker, I told residents in Queens, N.Y., that they would now be required to separate household trash into eight different color-coded bins. I can't imagine someone being more passionate about any world controversy than the gentleman who was incensed about a bin devoted to "poultry waste." "How," he asked, "am I going to eat enough chicken in two weeks to fill that up?"

◆ ◆ ◆

MY FIRST APPEARANCE on "Candid Camera" came when I was three and Dad was still trying to figure out how best to use the ingenious concept he had invented—first on radio in 1947, and the following year on television. (The show ran on TV in 1948 with the radio name "Candid Microphone," because back then television was such a media stepchild no one ever thought to add "Camera" to the show's title.) My assignment was to stand on a busy street corner in Manhattan, working as a shoeshine boy who charged $10 per shoe. I guess the idea was to see how adults would react to such a young and audacious entrepreneur. Alas, back then they didn't save raw footage or even finished shows. My piece ran once, and was tossed in the trash (a line critics could have had fun with later in my career).

It wasn't until my early teens that I got a chance to meaningfully participate—but only when the job involved something that no one except the boss's son could be commanded to do. One such sequence was shot in Seattle, where Dad constructed an upside down room. Everything that should have

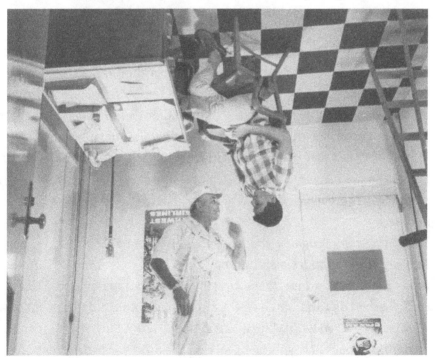

WELL HUNG: Getting final instructions from Dad, while already feeling faint.

been on the floor—desk, chair, lamp, etc.—was bolted to the ceiling. All that was needed to complete the illusion was someone nimble enough, and foolish enough, to hang upside down behind the desk and conduct brief conversations with visitors. Brevity was necessary because after a very short time blood would rush to my head and I'd start to feel faint. Three strong guys ran in and walked me around until I was able to pass the equivalent of a sobriety test. Then they put me back on the ceiling—held in place by only a flimsy auto seatbelt. This went on for eight hours.

The worst part about my uncomfortable day was that nothing usable ever happened. Strangers came in to the room (seeking tourist information), took one look at this crazy situation, and experienced *cognitive dissonance*—a psychological term meaning "nothing funny here"—and ran out. A few seconds of the footage eventually ran on "Candid Camera" in a collection labeled "Things We Tried That Flopped."

BETTER RESULTS came the following year in a "Candid Camera" sequence shot at a Manhattan art gallery that was closed for the day. The "subjects" (our term for the unsuspecting participants) were janitors, tasked with cleaning the showroom, where a statue of a Roman soldier was on display. The statue, played by an actor covered with white paint, would move slightly to startle the worker. My job that day was to carry equipment, get coffee for the crew, take notes and, for several hours, watch as the sequence failed miserably. The actor couldn't keep his eyes closed and still manage to be "caught" at just the right time.

Among the toughest challenges when a sequence just isn't working is deciding whether to try a second day and risk losing even more money, or abandon the gag and write off the cost of one failed day. Dad opted to roll the dice on a second day and, almost as an afterthought, told me to play the statue.

I was covered with white makeup that dried to look like plaster. After a few agonizing hours I began to suspect that the prop guy had run out of makeup and substituted actual plaster. Anyway, I was quite white and very stiff. I had to stand completely still on a small pedestal, eyes closed, and somehow guess when the cleaning man was nearby, but not looking my way, in order to poke him with my spear. Producer Chet Dowling was posing as the gallery owner. He brought each janitor into the area where I was positioned and gave simple instructions about cleaning, with warnings about not disturbing the "valuable artifacts." After a few wasted tries, I poked a fellow who seemed to be properly startled and mystified. I shifted position slightly. Then I kicked him gently in the rear end. His reactions were perfect. A few moves later I let him catch me.

Since the gag had never gotten this far the first day, no thought had been given to what the statue would say if caught. I blurted a story about how my friend and I cooked up a scheme to make money by "selling" me to the gallery. Incredibly, he swallowed it so I pushed ahead, complaining that I was tired from standing rigidly for so long. Would he mind filling in for a while? Lo and behold, he took my spear and climbed onto the pedestal. I said I was going out for something to eat and, "Whatever you do, don't move. Because if he comes back and sees you moving, you're in big trouble!"

I circled around to the rear door and into the back room where the crew was choking down laughs and wondering what to do next. It was decided that Lou Tyrrell, a director on the show, would play the part of an interested buyer. He walked in, examined the quivering cleaning man and offered to buy the "statue."

At this point we had practically shot enough for a feature film. I went back in and told him it was "Candid Camera" and—thank the TV gods—he began smiling. We didn't shoot another foot of film. It was one of those rare instances where we couldn't possibly do any better, even if we shot for another month. So we headed back to the office to tell Dad what had happened.

During this period in the early sixties the sequences were shot on 16mm film. The footage would have to be sent to a lab for processing overnight. What we saw the next day was hilarious and even better than we thought. Still, Dad was worried. He watched the film over and over, and each time he asked Chet and Lou if they were certain that this sweet man was fully sane. If, kidding aside, a Candid subject was actually mentally impaired, Dad would never have allowed the footage to be broadcast, no matter how funny it was.

Finally, my father did something that had never been done before, or since, in our show's long history. He phoned the man and asked if he would submit to a "chat" with a psychologist. After the exam, the doctor came to the office with his report.

"So?" asked Dad. "He's nuts, right?" "No, Allen," he replied. "I believe he's perfectly sane. But after hearing about your little stunt, I'm beginning to have my doubts about you."

"CANDID CAMERA" IS BUILT ON THE PREMISE that anyone in America might be caught, so I've done a lot of traveling. Indeed, my crew and I probably log many more miles than in Dad's day because the public now expects it, and technology allows it. Back in the forties and fifties just about every "Candid Camera" sequence was filmed within a few blocks of Times Square. The pitch to viewers wasn't *you* could be caught; rather, you'll enjoy seeing *other people* caught, even if they're all in New York City. In the sixties that began to change, although there were still many scenes shot close to Manhattan. Yonkers, the medium-sized city a few miles to the north, often served as a generic substitute for much of the U.S. when the show needed to get "out of town."

As ratings and the production budget grew, Dad began traveling across America as well as to several foreign locales. A major motivator was the show's new slogan first broadcast in 1961: "Don't be surprised if sometime, somewhere, someplace when you least expect it, someone steps up to you and says: Smile! You're on Candid Camera."

No one in particular gets credit for that line, although it grew out of earlier phrases dreamed up by a fellow named Al Slep, a family friend and talented PR man. Al coined: "Until next time, you go your way and we'll go your way too, with the Candid Camera!" He also wrote that people photographed by the show were, "caught in the act of being themselves." In the sixties, the staff was seeking to mix in the word "smile" to counter negative comments by critics who kept writing that "Candid Camera" was *mean-spirited*. A slogan emphasizing that getting caught was worth smiling about gradually helped change the perception.

♦ ♦ ♦

GETTING OUT OF NEW YORK CITY brought new energy to the show. In Raleigh, North Carolina, for example, Dad engaged a local gentleman in a dry cleaning shop about the pronunciation of the words "all" and "oil." When spoken in certain parts of the South they sound exactly the same, at least to visitors from the North. Over the course of several minutes the guy said "oil" and "all" dozens of times, with no discernable difference.

Nowadays cities look so alike that we have to be careful when we're on the road. Airport terminals, rental car counters, restaurant chains, all tend to look the same. If you've seen one Embassy Suites, you've seen them all—which, come to think of it, is probably the crux of the Embassy Suites marketing plan—but it leaves you wondering what else a city has to offer. Our goal is to never allow viewers to feel like zombified business travelers, trapped in look-a-like surroundings. The absolute worst situation for us would be to journey to, say, Phoenix to shoot a gag about eating, and decide to do it at a Subway restaurant in a strip mall, next to a Gap and a PetSmart. Unless there happened to be a window in the background providing a view of a giant cactus across the street, then the trip to Phoenix is pretty much a waste of time and money.

On the road I try to shoot more gags outdoors. I also look for sequences that tap into issues or quirks specific to a region. For instance, I once read that according to some kind of survey, Nebraska is one of the most *boring* places in America. (I'll never understand surveys like that. Whom did they ask, people living in Nebraska? Or was this the opinion of New Yorkers and Californians?) Anyway, a few days later, we were at the state capitol in Lincoln, where Governor Ben Nelson let us shoot a gag in his private office and, even better, he agreed to do the entire gag himself. (Who says Nebraskans don't know how to have fun?)

The staff brought in local citizens one at a time, explaining that the governor wanted to get feedback about a pressing issue. Nelson said he'd hired a marketing firm to create excitement about the state, and their advice was to get rid of the name Nebraska. We fed him a few possibilities for new names that sounded ultra-modern such as "Zenmar" and "Quentron." One woman said she'd actually given the matter some thought and believed a good name would be "Aksarben." Apparently Nelson had thought about it, too. He knew right away that Aksarben is Nebraska spelled backwards.

Another woman really set the governor straight. "I like things the way they are," she said. "I've always thought if the world were to end tomorrow, the best place to be would be Nebraska because it wouldn't happen here until ten years later."

◆ ◆ ◆

A FEW YEARS AFTER THAT VISIT I got Nebraska on my brain again when I watched a TV program about "crop circles," the neatly formed circular patterns in cornfields, created by pivoting irrigation systems. I learned they have a lot of these in Nebraska, so producer Kate McNamara and I flew to Scottsbluff and pretended to be UFO investigators from Washington. We wore blue coveralls with D.U.H. printed in big black letters on the back, which stood for *Department of Unexplained Happenings*. We were armed with aerial photos of "mysterious" circles in the cornfields that we said raised serious concerns about alien visitors.

This is probably a good time to comment about whether working on "Candid Camera" is *fun*. I'm asked that a lot. Certainly, working on our TV show—I'd say just about any TV show—is more fun than a lot of other jobs. (Except Mike Rowe's "Dirty Jobs" show on the Discovery Channel, where one week Mike's cleaning sewers and the next he's learning how to squeeze excrement out of baby chickens.) So, sure, what we do is fun. But when people are depending on you, and a lot of money is at stake, and deadlines are creating enormous stress, then even the most pleasant job becomes hard work. But mostly, like on this beautiful sunny day in far western Nebraska, I can't imagine anything more fun than my job.

Wearing dark sunglasses and FBI-style earpieces, Kate and I stepped effortlessly into our parts by simply convincing ourselves that we really *were* investigating UFOs. Of course, it didn't hurt that most people in Scottsbluff actually believe there *are* ETs in the cornfields. At least that's what we concluded after chatting with a few farmers. The highlight was our visit to the home of Mrs. Gay Luce, who we met at the edge of her field:

ME: *We're from Washington, D.C.*

MRS. LUCE: *What's happening?*

ME: *We have aerial recognizance photos that lead us to believe there may be UFOs here.*

MRS. LUCE: *Is that right?*

ME: *Yes, UFOs that have landed in the cornfield.*

MRS. LUCE: *Is that right?*

KATE: *We were checking your cornfield to see if there's anything unusual here.*

ME: *Have you had any unexplained happenings?*

MRS. LUCE: *I just moved in.*

ME: *Well, the people who left, were they scared off by the aliens?*

MRS. LUCE: *They might have been.*

ME: *Have you witnessed anything unusual?*

MRS. LUCE: *I think we had UFOs where I lived before.*

ME: *Where was that, ma'am?*

MRS. LUCE: *Just west of town.*

KATE: *This town?*

MRS. LUCE: *Yes.*

ME: *We don't want to alarm you, but we'd like you to report to our office in Washington, D.C. anything that might happen here to confirm our suspicions about UFOs.*

MRS. LUCE: *You bet!*

Just then, a local police car pulled into the driveway. Apparently, one of the farmers we'd visited earlier became worried that Kate and I posed more of a threat than visitors from space and had dialed 911 as soon as we left. (Having police interrupt one of our gags might seem like a problem, but it's actually something I hope for and have practiced how to handle. So when the officer arrived, Todd Simon knew to keep his camera rolling no matter what transpired.)

ME: *You see these photos of circles in the fields?*

MRS. LUCE: *Yes. (She spots the police car.)*

ME: *Apparently the local police have pulled up. They must have gotten the report as well. There are agents and police swarming all over the place today.*

MRS. LUCE: *I'm surprised they're not all out here, actually.*
(To the officer.) They think there are UFOs in the field.

ME: *You see this picture?*

COP: *That's a center pivot.*

ME: *A center what?*

COP: *Pivot. Irrigation pivot.*

ME: *Our department thought these pictures confirmed there were UFOs.*

MRS. LUCE: *This wouldn't be like a Candid Camera thing would it?*

ME: *You're exactly right! There's the camera right there.*

MRS. LUCE: *Are you serious? You guys are nuts!*

(To the officer.) Are you in on this?

COP: *No, ma'am, I'm not.*

ME: *I'm Peter Funt from Candid Camera. This is Kate McNamara.*

MRS. LUCE: *(Laughing.) You guys scared me to death!*

Mrs. Luce was scared to death by Kate and me. UFOs didn't worry her so much.

◆ ◆ ◆

ONE OF THE RISKS that comes with shooting on the road is we have even less control of our surroundings than we do at home, which isn't very much to begin with. Once we were shooting a gag at a motel in Albuquerque, where I played the desk clerk, checking people in. My idea was to quote very low room rates, but then gradually allow customers to discover that everything else was extra: bars of soap, 10 cents each; hangers, 15 cents for wire and 35 cents for wood; a mint on your pillow, 5 cents, and yada, yada. It was going well until two bad things happened unexpectedly.

I was explaining to a woman that hand towels were 50 cents each and bath towels were a dollar. Her husband was across the small lobby near a window in front of which we had placed a large cactus to block the light that had been streaming in. (Also to provide visual proof that we were in the Southwest.) I don't know the horticultural name for this particular cactus, but it's the kind that is covered with spikes, sort of like large sewing needles—definitely something you wouldn't want to touch. The guy waiting for his wife never touched the cactus with his hands. What he did do was lean back in his chair until he fell into the plant. I heard a scream and looked up to see the man leap to his feet with the entire cactus clinging to his back. He began to run around the lobby the way movie characters do when an animal grabs them from behind and hangs on for a fun-filled romp. In this case, no one was laughing. We stopped tape, pulled the cactus off the man, and spent about 20 minutes using pliers from camerman Todd Simon's tool kit to extract needles from the guy's tail. Mercifully the couple was nice about it and took us up on our offer of a free dinner at one of Albuquerque's best restaurants.

What I didn't realize as we resumed the shoot was that this must have been *Cursed Couples' Day* at this particular motel, because a short while later the scene was basically recreating itself as I told a woman that wakeup calls were 75 cents while her boyfriend paced around the lobby, just close enough to hear everything I was saying. "Valet parking is ten dollars," I said all too cheerfully. "No," she said flatly, "we'll just park ourselves."

"Sure. Self-parking is eight dollars."

I guess that did it, because without uttering a word the boyfriend picked up a wrought iron floor lamp, swung it over his head, and charged toward the desk where I was standing with such fury that you would have thought he had a cactus stuck to his rear end. I've told this story dozens of times in public appearances, and it always goes like this:

Todd, who's about 6-foot-4, was only five feet away behind a screen. Brian the audio engineer was right with him. We had a production assistant nearby, plus two hotel employees watching everything. But what I learned that day was, when a guy comes at you swinging an iron floor lamp, you're pretty much on your own.

That always gets a laugh. But the fact is, as fast as the incident began, it just sort of stopped. The woman did what she could to calm her boyfriend. Alas, a meal at the restaurant where the cactus couple was dining wouldn't work with these two. They rejected dinner, and a free night at the motel. Worse, they kept leaving and then coming back in the middle of our work with demands about free hangers or something. (I guess they never caught on to the actual "joke" part of what we were doing.)

HAVING SHOT "CANDID CAMERA" SEQUENCES in all 50 states, I'm often asked which parts of the country are funniest. Where do we get the best reactions? Much of it has to do, of course, with the type of gag we're doing. For example, consider various movie theater gags we've done and where we believed the would work best:

"Alphabetical Movie Line"—Patrons waiting outside a busy theater were told by our guy that "to be fair" everyone should line up alphabetically by last name, regardless of when they arrived. This gag really had to be done in a big city, and New York was ideal. It wouldn't have been funny at, say, a suburban mall location where the lines are shorter and customers tend to be more patient.

"Reserved Seating Only"—Moviegoers at a sparsely attended show are informed that they must buy tickets online in advance. Here, New York would have been a poor choice; it makes too much sense. Instead, we shot the piece in Stowe, Vermont, where a dozen or so customers, having braved 10-degree weather, were stunned to find out they could not purchase tickets at the door.

"Recycled Popcorn"—At the concession stand, we pretended to fill new popcorn bags from older half-empty bags that were "picked up by ushers after the last show." This struck us as a California-type gag and we shot it in the surfing community of Santa Cruz, where concerns about hygiene, but also a strong commitment to recycling, created the perfect conflict.

3 / BAD DEALS, GREAT WHEELS

BEFORE MY FATHER PASSED AWAY in 1999 I promised him I'd always honor his cardinal rule: We Funts shall never publish the real names of people who have screwed us or stolen from us, even though in years to come they will be easily Googled.

Dad was talented, fortunate and occasionally unlucky.

In 1969 an accountant, whose real name was not Mort Zimmerstein, stole all of Dad's money, more than $2.5 million, and when caught he checked into a seedy Manhattan hotel and killed himself. (I guess if you're intending to kill yourself you're not going to stress over the quality of the breakfast buffet.) Mort had donated a significant portion of the embezzled funds to a Jewish synagogue on Long Island, so Dad drove out there to get his money back. As he waited in the lobby to meet with the directors he noticed a fancy plaque honoring Mort for his generosity. Dad made his case and then the group met briefly before handing down its decision: We are unable to return any of the money; however, we have decided to put your name on the plaque.

In 1991 a television distributor not named Blurt Rosen embezzled more than $1 million from Dad by selling episodes of "Candid Camera" overseas and falsifying the receipts. The scheme grew worse when a French TV station made unauthorized copies of the shows and shipped them back to the U.S., where they turned up on the E! Entertainment cable channel. The copies were so poor that they looked like VHS wedding videos that had been recorded over a school recital that had been recorded over a bar mitzvah. When Dad informed E!'s people that they had (apparently) been duped, they said they had receipts to prove they had paid the French crooks—as if that mattered—and refused to stop running the shows. The case went to what's known as binding arbitration, in which a retired judge listens to both sides while trying to avoid dozing off, orders an especially expensive deli platter for lunch, and then issues a Solomon-like ruling. In this case: Blurt would admit to no wrong-doing, but he agreed to return the master tapes—which turned up outside the San Fernando Valley warehouse of a porn producer not nicknamed Tricky Dick.

I've spent much of my career following in Dad's footsteps which was not always a good thing. In 2007 my bookkeeper, Zelda Quantum (not her real name), robbed me of $250,000 by using my company's Mastercard to charge clothing, jewelry and trips to Vegas. This infuriated me, of course, but not as much as the fact that I had paid a top accounting firm in Monterey, California, to vet Zelda before I hired her. They gave her a glowing report—overlooking, among other things, that she had once robbed a bank in Carmel. She confessed to stealing from me and was sentenced to two years in prison. After her trial I asked the assistant D.A. how I should go about recovering my money. He laughed heartily.

DAD HAD A WEAKNESS for expensive cars. Initially, he favored Cadillac convertibles but when his show climbed to the top of the ratings in the mid-sixties he bought himself a Bentley in a deep bronze color. It was a magnificent but wildly pretentious car, with touches like polished wood folding tables in the backseat. Fortunately, by the time this car arrived I was away at college and didn't have to be seen riding in it, but my sister Patty and brother John were not so lucky. They had to endure being driven to school while hiding on the floor in the back, begging Dad to stop a few blocks from school so they could jump out and walk the rest of the way.

The Bentley had quite a storied run. Once Dad was stopped at a light on West 55th Street in Manhattan, when a guy on foot banged on the window to ask about the car. It was Muhammad Ali. As a result of the encounter, Ali wound up performing as a guest in three "Candid Camera" episodes. At about the same time, my parents' marriage was on the rocks and Dad was falling for his secretary, Marilyn. Late one night they consummated their relationship in the back of the Bentley, parked under an overpass in the Bronx, where they were interrupted by a cop. Like Ali, the cop immediately recognized Dad. Unlike Ali, he did not ask to appear on television—although he did accept one hundred dollars for his discretion.

Meanwhile, I came home for Thanksgiving, eager to visit my college girlfriend, Sydney Isaacson, and meet her parents in Great Neck, a town on Long Island about 45 miles from our house in Croton-on-Hudson in Westchester County. I had spent months at school trying to persuade Sydney that, despite Dad's showbiz success, my family lived a simple, down-to-earth life. So, the day after Thanksgiving Dad hands me the keys to the Bentley. I pleaded with him to let me drive his Jeep but he wouldn't hear of it. He had some kind of fantasy going about how impressed Sydney and her parents would be when they saw the Bentley in their driveway. (He was unaware that at the University of Denver Sydney drove a yellow Corvette.) I don't think I've ever been so nervous as I was steering Dad's gleaming mega-vehicle over the Whitestone Bridge. Sydney insisted we drive to every local hangout, and I noticed that a lot of people in Great Neck owned luxury cars—some of which were so luxurious that they made the Bentley seem like a Mercury Montego. (As part of my research for this book I read the Wikipedia entry for Great Neck: "One of the most affluent towns in the country." I also learned that many famous people have lived there, among them Fred Schwartz, "Furrier, Philanthropist and Television Pitchman.")

As problematic as the Bentley was for everyone except Dad, the Jeep was also a constant source of agita for Patty, John and me. Dad had purchased 50 acres of woodlands next to our house, and weekends were devoted to clearing trails through the forest. One day the Jeep became stuck in deep mud and we spent several hours trying to get it out with a winch on the back of the Jeep and a steel cable wrapped around a tree. The next time we ran into this type of trouble we winched the vehicle free only to have it slide into more mud, requiring more winching. Soon the three of us made a horrible discovery about Dad that affected our weekends for years to come: He enjoyed winching more than clearing trails. He drove recklessly through the woods for hours hoping the Jeep would accidentally become stuck.

In 1962 Dad brought home a silver Mercedes-Benz 220SE Cabriolet convertible. This was a hard car to hate—even for those of us who opposed ostentatious forms of transportation. One day he parked it in front of the barn at the far end of our property where we kept three horses. As he talked with Mom outside one of the stalls, and as Patty, John and I sneezed due to our hay allergies, the Mercedes began rolling, slowly at first, toward a steep hill leading down to the woods. Dad dashed toward it, but stopped as the car picked up speed and bounced down the incline and across a pasture until it smashed into one of our favorite winching trees. We watched helplessly as the 220SE burst into flames and roasted to its core.

This was not the only incident at our barn, which might have had some kind of curse. One evening, when Dad was working late in Manhattan, we looked up from dinner to see a large ball of flame rising over the area where the barn was located—the equivalent of two blocks from our house. I jumped up and ran to the barn which, by the time I got there, was what news reporters describe as fully involved. Without thinking, I went into each stall to rescue the horses. One, named Gal, was burning. I got the three frightened horses into a corral and threw a blanket over Gal (she survived, as did the others). Mom, Patty and John stood with me as the barn burned to the ground. Roughly 20 minutes later, with the smoke dissipating, members of the Croton Volunteer Fire Department roared onto the scene.

The department, located in the center of town about five miles away, was known for its barbecues, tag sales and sponsorship of a Little League team plus, of course, battling occasional blazes. The volunteers were called to action by the sound of a loud horn atop the fire station, at which time one or two guys would drive the town's fire engine, while the rest of the respondents sped to the scene in private cars or on motorcycles. This arrangement resulted in a dozen or so able-bodied firefighters arriving at our house, along with about 20 younger "concerned citizens," or "JD's" as they were known in town, who, learning that the call was at Allen Funt's estate, felt compelled to rush over for a look. It was kind of like what realtors refer to as an open house. The group was so large that Mom nearly ran out of lemonade.

Looking back, it was a good thing that the fire was out by the time the volunteers arrived because they had no water. Our house was miles from any hydrants and what little plumbing there was in the barn had been fully fried. So, the volunteers toured our property while asking probing questions about the fire such as: "How did it start?"

Dad with Gal in Croton before the barn burned down.

4 / RED HILL

CROTON IS A VILLAGE on the Hudson River, about 30 miles north of New York City. Dad moved us there from a small Eastside apartment soon after I was born, having found a bargain-priced house on Mount Airy Road with large white gates in front, and cleverly named by the previous owners *White Gates.* (It was sort of like a property I saw recently with the catchy name *Gate Opens Out.*) In the fifties Croton was populated mostly by stone masons, railroad workers and Communists. The masons arrived in 1892 to build the some-what-famous Croton Dam. The rail workers were employed by the New York Central Railroad at the nearby Harmon Yards. No one seems to know why so many Communists settled in Croton, although I've heard speculation that they enjoyed the company of masons and the convenience of a well-maintained railroad. I'm not sure how many were real card-carrying Commies; most were people who believed in radical concepts like equal rights. Today such folks are known as *moderates.*

(Wikipedia: "Croton was a popular location for American communists, socialists and other radicals and many important artists and writers. This gave the Mt. Airy area in Croton the nickname 'Red Hill.'")

AS A KID I used to sit on the floor in our living room and marvel at my father's snoring while he slept on the couch. I hadn't yet encountered any-one else who snored, so it seemed to be Dad's unique talent—and he was darn good at it. Dad drove each morning to his Manhattan office, and usually made it back in time for dinner. The best days were when he chased down a Good Humor ice cream truck on the drive home and purchased treats, although he frequently consumed all the ice cream before reaching our driveway. My mother, Evelyn Funt, stayed home and took care of her three kids as well as a large property with five buildings that started as ten acres and grew, thanks to various purchases, to be 65. Mom was as talented and perky as Laura Petrie; she was as loving as June Cleaver, and in our home she often caught the harsh end of domestic disputes but rose above them, just like Alice Kramden. Looking back, I guess I watched a lot of television. Sunday nights were particularly exciting: We rushed through dinner to watch "Lassie," "Ed Sullivan," and the rest of the CBS lineup, followed at 10 by "Candid Camera." I absolutely loved everything my father did on the show and I inched as close to the TV set as I could, picturing myself as host. Funny thing: it never seemed to be my father up there on the screen, but rather some *television guy*. The man I called Dad was right there on the couch, capable of falling asleep during any TV show ever broadcast, except "Candid Camera."

When it came to building things in and around our house, Dad was what they called *handy*. He could do just about anything with power tools, and had a basement workshop full of equipment. Trouble was, the basement had a low ceiling and no windows. Right after breakfast on Saturdays and Sundays he would begin sawing and grinding, filling the basement with sawdust and smoke. When any of us dared to venture down there we were invariably roped into "helping," which really meant "watching" while coughing for hours at a time. Whenever Dad was between projects he would remodel our spare room upstairs to fit whatever interested the kids at the moment—a "general store," the "deck of a boat," a "spaceship." We enjoyed these fantasy setups almost as much as he did.

MANY OF MY FONDEST MEMORIES of growing up in Croton revolve around Christmas. In early December we'd go to the vacant lot in Harmon where trees were sold, and each year I heard my father ask the same thing: "Don't you have any bigger trees?" We bought the tallest tree they had, tied it to the roof of the Jeep, and listened to Dad insist, "Don't worry, we'll make it fit in the living room." Year to year, as the trees got bigger but the height of our ceiling stayed the same, Dad would cut an increasingly large piece off the top. (He refused to cut from the bottom, "because that's where the best branches are.") By the time I was ten our tree had no shape whatsoever; it was basically a large cylinder. Besides this tree problem, Dad's other weakness at Christmas was that he couldn't wait to show us our gifts. He'd bring something home a week before Christmas and start hinting about it at dinner. By the time dessert was finished we were already tired of playing with it.

The year I turned eight he gave us a regulation-size trampoline. We set it up in the living room which had a ten-foot ceiling. Do the math: the trampoline's legs were about three feet off the ground . . . I was five feet tall . . . leaving roughly two feet of clearance between my head and the ceiling. I didn't have to bounce much to be at serious risk.

Not wanting to move the trampoline out into the snow, and not having any rooms with higher ceilings, Dad decided I should wear a helmet. However, there were very few helmets back then. The Little Leaguers wore a type of padded earmuffs that didn't cover the top of the head at all. There was no such thing as a bicycle helmet; even motorcyclists wouldn't be caught dead wearing one (although with their heads uncovered, being caught dead seemed like a real possibility). Always resourceful, Dad had me wear a burgundy English equestrian helmet. Once protected, I persisted in jumping as high as possible, trying to smash my head into the ceiling. By Christmas morning the trampoline had already been moved into storage.

At least I got to play with that gift for a few days, which wasn't the case with the Lionel train set. This was in the mid-fifties when "Candid Camera" was not in production ("resting" as TV people say). Without discussion, Dad took the train set to the vacant room above our three-car garage and began to design—for himself—one of the world's most complex layouts. For the next four months he emerged only for meals and sleep. The project had three levels, with cities and towns, mountains and lakes, plus miles of wire. At times we'd all get lured into helping. I remember nights when Mom and my aunt Dorothy would be on their knees under the table for many hours, attaching tiny tags to the maze of wires.

Then one day the train project was finished. Without the challenge of designing and building it, Dad quickly lost interest.

One gift that changed my life—the oddest present imaginable—was a Ditto machine. A what? A Ditto machine, a piece of office equipment that was a low-cost competitor to mimeograph copying machines. These "spirit duplicators" used noxious fluid and a special mixture of wax and ink. They were popular among teachers for churning out copies of a fact sheet or quiz, while also producing a pretty good buzz if you inhaled enough of the fumes.

Mom and Dad sought to encourage my interest in journalism by buying me all sorts of stuff with which to print my own little newspapers. I soon owned two typewriters: an Olympia portable and an old Royal that had once been used to create price tags in a clothing store. Its keys contained only capital letters, but each was about a half-inch tall—giving me a second font style for headlines.

Production soared to even greater heights with the gift I received on my 16th birthday: a Thermo-Fax machine. This table-top device, developed circa 1950 by the 3M Company, was an early competitor to Xerox. It used heat to produce copies of any original, so long as the original contained carbon-based ink. The remarkable part for me, and the reason I was so eager to get this device, was that in addition to making ordinary copies a Thermo-Fax could also create Ditto masters. Now I could type on plain paper and add clip-art from almost any printed source, and then run the whole thing through my Thermo-Fax to produce a Ditto master. (TMI? Sorry.)

My first publishing effort with these machines was called the *Election News*, a one-shot I produced the day after the presidential election of 1964. I stayed up all night gleaning results from TV and radio, and illustrating my roundups with photos of the candidates clipped from newspapers. I Dittoed 50 copies of a ten-page paper with the boxcar headline: LBJ WINS. Alas, there wasn't much *news* in that. Lyndon Johnson scored an overwhelming victory over Republican Barry Goldwater, an outcome that had been clear by dinnertime the night before.

Hoping to sell to commuters, I placed a chair borrowed from our kitchen at the Oscawana railroad station with a stack of *Election News* copies, and a small cardboard box for payments (25 cents) via the honor system. I even put a few quarters in the box to give customers the idea. Meanwhile, at nearby Crugers station, I stood at the boarding area shouting: "Latest election news! Complete results!" One woman gave me a quarter, but explained as she scurried to her train that she really didn't need the paper.

Back at Oscawana, the best thing that happened was that none of my own quarters was stolen. *Election News* sold a total of zero copies.

In Cub Scouts I got a merit badge for penmanship.

IF YOU PICTURE, say, Sunset Boulevard in Hollywood, then you have a pretty good idea of what the village of Croton was not like. Yet, Red Hill had a few random showbiz residents. Living next door to us was Robert "Shad" Northshield, the innovative producer of NBC's "Huntley-Brinkley Report" and later creator of CBS's dignified "Sunday Morning" magazine show. Our neighbor on the other side was Peter Strauss, born the same year as me, whose acting accomplishments, most notably in the role of Rudy Jordache in ABC's "Rich Man, Poor Man," earned him the unofficial title, "King of the Network Mini-Series." And a few miles down the road from our place was the unusual circular house that CBS built as a weekend retreat for the legendary Jackie Gleason.

One Sunday afternoon Gleason and his girlfriend, who went only by the name Honey, paid us a visit. Leaving no doubt about how he earned his reputation as a heavy drinker, the man TV viewers best remember as Ralph Kramden in "The Honeymooners," barreled into our driveway in a blue Cadillac convertible. The driveway was steep, winding, and about a quarter-mile long. On the left as you entered was a concrete wall, roughly two-feet high and almost two-feet wide that served as protection against the precipitous drop on that side. Gleason managed to hit this wall in such a way that the entire left side of his car's chassis hung up on top, while the car's right side remained balanced on its tires on the pavement. Not willing to concede the problem, nor interested in trying to back up, Gleason rammed that Cadillac all the way up our driveway—creating a deafening sound, and leaving a 1,000-foot blue streak on the wall.

He said hello and, without even mentioning what happened, asked Mom for a drink. After some conversation with Dad he lifted up my brother John, who was three or four at the time, plopped him on his lap and proceeded to "hypnotize" him. *Terrorize* would be a better word for it. After John finally squirmed free, Gleason said goodbye.

Holding a drink with one hand and the steering wheel with the other, he somehow managed to navigate back down the driveway without damaging the wall, or Honey.

5 / GOOD SPORTS

I EXCELLED AT BASEBALL, tennis and golf—a problem during high school, because all three sports are played in the spring. Football, I was not good at.

At Croton-Harmon High I tried out for football and was named third-string quarterback on the junior varsity team, a position the NFL refers to as *Clipboard Holder*. We wore the varsity's hand-me-down uniforms. By the time my jersey reached me it had shrunk to about half its original size, but my pants remained the same as when previously worn by a 250-pound lineman. We were instructed to find old inner tubes and cut them into thigh bands to hold up our pants. Fully dressed, I looked like a caterpillar.

I was never what players call *in the loop*. After three grueling weeks of practice I had managed to learn one play: Dive right 34, in which the running back, Vinnie Chicarelli, took a handoff and plunged into the 4-hole between the guard and tackle on the right side.

Our first game was at Hendrick Hudson High. Trailing 28-0 in the third quarter, the coach put me in. Naturally, I called "Dive right 34." I took the snap and turned to my right, hoping to find Chic running full steam. Instead I saw a tower of Hen-Hud players, the shortest of whom must have been 6-3. As I crashed to the ground I attempted a lateral in the direction of the 4-hole and a swarm of Hen-Hud guys jumped on the ball. The following day I turned in my uniform and decided to wait for basketball to begin.

I made the freshman basketball squad but in January was ruled ineligible due to *le défaut* in Madame Donzella's French class. This wasn't a surprise since the only French I knew after four months was *la plume de ma tante*, and there's a limit to how many times you can write "the pen of my aunt" on a midterm exam. My best skill in French class was competing with friends in "taking a bow." This meant standing and bowing when Miss Donzella was writing on the board, and holding the position for as long as possible before she turned around. Years later my wife Amy, who speaks fluent French and Italian, informed me, "You have no facility for foreign language." It was what linguists refer to as an *aha moment.*

In spring I managed to regain eligibility and became a true slugging star on the freshman baseball team. I've always loved baseball, as did my father, who at times took it too seriously. When I was ten he became the only parent ever banned by the Croton Little League. This occurred following his third offense of yelling at an umpire—not groaning or even booing, mind you, but actually *screaming.* Next game, freed from the pressure of having to worry about Dad's passion, I homered in my first at-bat. When I came up again, a high and inside pitch was called a strike. Immediately, loud honking erupted from the parking lot. Everyone turned and saw that the noise was coming from a chocolate brown Lincoln Continental convertible—the only one of its kind in Croton, perhaps in all of Westchester County.

Dad spent the remainder of the season in exile, tooting his own horn.

IN THE 1960S CBS insisted that "Candid Camera" have occasional guest stars, even though most celebrities didn't appreciate the show's unique approach on locations: no dressing rooms, no makeup, no craft service and, of course, no script. Dad figured he could tolerate guests if they were athletes he admired. Jackie Robinson co-hosted an episode because Dad wanted to meet the Dodgers' legend. Basketball star Jerry Lucas was also a guest; Muhammad Ali, as I noted earlier, made three appearances.

The ballplayer Dad and I most wanted to meet was Mickey Mantle. This was arranged in 1960 when Mickey and teammate Yogi Berra had an off-day on the Yankees' schedule and agreed to do a "Candid Camera" gag at a golf course in New Jersey. I was allowed to be there as a *go-fer*, but mainly so I could be in the company of a man whose batting stance I had practiced for countless hours in front of my bedroom mirror. (To this day all my passwords use the number "7"—which was Mickey's number on the Yankees.)

Mickey is photogenic. I'm numb. Yogi can't find the camera.

The idea, at least when the day began, was to have two caddies (Mickey and Yogi) give golfers heavy doses of unwanted advice. It was a mess. Mickey was so shy he could barely speak; Yogi didn't mind speaking, but you couldn't quite understand anything he said. After all, Yogi is the guy who observed, "90 percent of the game is half mental." During the first three takes, Mickey sat on a bench trying to stay out of the picture, while Yogi said something about keeping one's eye on the ball, during which time the players hit their shots and walked off. Normally this type of stuff would drive my father nuts but Dad calmly changed the stunt to be: Two caddies tell golfers they're doing everything wrong and one grabs a club to show how it should be done. This version was only tried once, but I can report that without warming up, and using a persimmon driver of the period, Mickey hit the ball over 300 yards. It just wasn't very funny. Desperate to get something usable, Dad stepped into the scene to sell golfers "balls used earlier today by Mickey Mantle and Yogi Berra." One woman agreed to pay 50 cents for a ball, so Dad introduced her to the players, at which point she said, "Then I'll give you three dollars."

Years later, in an interview with Bryant Gumbel, Yogi was asked to try some word association. The first thing Gumbel said was, "Mickey Mantle," to which Yogi replied, "What about him?"

◆ ◆ ◆

AS A KID Yogi played American Legion baseball in St. Louis, and that's where the "Candid Camera" crew went a few years after the golf fiasco to see how mothers of young players would fare as sports announcers on KMOX Radio:

ANNOUNCER: Good afternoon ladies and gentlemen, and welcome again to a very exciting afternoon of baseball here at the Fairground Park. And here for a play-by-play description is Mrs. Barbara James.

MRS. JAMES: Good afternoon. Now at bat, we have a strike one, and who is our first batter up? Charlie Shapper, who plays right field normally. He's batting up. He's a left hooker. What do you call it when they play left-handed like that? Left-hander? Oh! It's going... Oh! It's an out. But it was a beautiful out, it was well caught. The pitcher is warming up, and that was, well, a nothing. What was that? That was a beautiful foul ball. But they're not hitting the ball. And now we're going to see what this pitcher does. Oh, he's going to walk it. Our batter gets to walk to first base. He sort of trotted as he went along...

Yogi would have loved it. I enjoyed it enough to try it again with KMOX 35 years later. I noticed that a few girls had joined the boys on the field, but the parents were still tongue-tied trying to describe the action. "Safe! Don't call him out. He's safe. Oh, he's out! No, he's safe. What are you?"

◆ ◆ ◆

NOW, MY TWO FAVORITE "Candid Camera" baseball experiences.

One: By the summer of 1990 I was co-hosting CBS specials and gradually taking over the family franchise. But Dad continued coming up with crazy ideas from left field—or, in this case, from the pitcher's mound. "What would happen if the catcher gave signals that the pitcher had never seen?" he wondered. "Would a pitch ever be thrown?" This was the type of idea I put in a category called, *Never Mention It Again and Hopefully Dad Will Forget About It.* We were in the final stages of production on a CBS special called "Candid Camera's Sporting Life," to be hosted by me and the sassy MTV veejay known as "Downtown" Julie Brown. We already had sequences about football (tackling dummy filled with shaving cream), tennis (rude doubles player criticizes her partner), golf (ball keeps falling off tee at driving range) and wrestling (guys try to persuade Allen the "sport" is not faked). Julie did a gag, too, in which she played a track star being timed by people using a stopwatch we rigged to run *backwards.* But Dad refused to let go of his idea about a catcher who gave signs the pitcher had never seen. I decided that disrupting an actual Major League game was out of the question, so I began calling various minor league teams. I was getting nowhere until I happened to phone the Jamestown Expos, back then the Class A affiliate of the Montreal Expos. They said "maybe." Maybe, provided I got permission from the parent club, the Jamestown manager, the New York-Penn League president, and the head of the umpires association. I suppose I should have been grateful they didn't insist on a letter from Governor Cuomo.

With all the approvals in finally hand, my crew and I flew to Buffalo, then drove to Jamestown's Municipal Stadium where, on this steamy night in August, the Expos were to play a doubleheader against the visiting Niagara Falls Rapids. We planned to do our gag at the start of the second game and during the first game I listened to the radio play-by-play on station WJTN. It occurred to me that the announcers, Pete Hubbell and Skip Pierce, were unaware of our stunt. I arranged for a feed of the radio broadcast to one of our tape machines.

The only people who knew what we were up to were Jamestown's manager, the real umpires, the public address announcer (whom I alerted to the gag minutes before it started) and the catcher, Dan Hargis. I met with Dan between games and we hid a wireless microphone under his chest protector. Then I ducked into the umpires' dressing room where I borrowed clothes from home plate ump Dave Steveley.

Here's why this loomed as the biggest disaster of my professional life: (1) We never do single-take gags—too risky, (2) We never let a participant in on it—the catcher might warn the pitcher, (3) The old stadium shook like crazy—our picture was bouncing up and down, (4) We didn't even have a real prank—the gag was based on Dad's random and basically unanswerable question.

I had received numerous warnings from the head of the umpires association as well as the league president that under no circumstances was an actual pitch to be thrown. Apparently all sorts of official records would be jeopardized if that happened—the leadoff batter might hit the pitch for a home run, then go on to break the all-time Class-A record for homers, leaving the record "tainted," and prompting calls for Congress to investigate the influence of "Candid Camera" on the achievement. Anyway, I said I'd try my best.

The Expos took the field to begin the second game. I strolled out to home plate and crouched behind Hargis as he caught warm-up pitches from Bob Baxter, a lefty. This is good, I thought, lefties are known to be a bit flaky (I read in the paper the next day that Baxter had gone to Harvard). SWOOSH, thump! OMG. So that's what a 93-mph fastball is like when you're practically leaning on the catcher's back.

"Play ball!" (Yes, I actually yelled it.)

The leadoff hitter for the Rapids stepped into the box, and Baxter looked in for the sign. He squinted and shook his head.

WJTN RADIO: There's confusion between the pitcher and the catcher, so let's get together. How can they get messed up with the first signal of the ballgame? This is ridiculous. I mean, this is the 48th game of the season, fans. If you don't have your signals straight by this time, I mean, you open up with a fastball, nine times out of ten.

Now Hargis was back behind the plate, wiggling his fingers in weird ways that Baxter had never seen. I called time and walked to the mound.

ME: What's going on here?

BAXTER: I can't understand the signals.

ME: How often do you guys play together?

HARGIS: You know the signals, let's go.

BAXTER: What? Those signals?

ME: Fellas, we've been out here five minutes and we haven't thrown a pitch yet.

WJTN: Maybe it's time for Baxter to get himself a set of glasses. They ought to take him to the optometrist because Hargis evidently is not the culprit.

ME: Okay, let's go!

WJTN: Baxter is ready. He's looking in, and he's still nodding no. Still nodding no. Still nodding no. It's as if he can't see or something. This is good news for the folks at the refreshment stand. You folks down there, you can stay in line. We haven't started the ballgame yet.

I called time again and motioned for manager Pat Daugherty to come out. Of course, he knew what was going on, so he put on a stern expression and walked with me to the mound.

DAUGHERTY: We don't have all night to play this game. What's happening, son?

BAXTER: He's not giving me the numbers.

DAUGHERTY: If he's not giving you the numbers, what is he doing?

BAXTER: He's giving me this, and this, and this...

ME: What does that mean?

BAXTER: I have no idea.

WJTN: We're still waiting for the first pitch. And time is called again. And the umpire is going out to talk to the pitcher. And he pointed. He's out of there! He threw Baxter out of the ballgame! He threw Baxter out of the ballgame. This is one of the most unbelievable things in the history of professional baseball, and we're seeing it right here!

ME: Bob, my name is Peter Funt and I do the "Candid Camera" television show, and we just put you on "Candid Camera!"

P-A ANNOUNCER: Good evening, ladies and gentlemen. We'd like you all to smile, because you and the Expos are on "Candid Camera!"

WJTN: It's "Candid Camera" folks, and we've all been taken. We walked right into it. Believe me, they did a great job.

Baxter was shaking, but he was smiling. The game was further delayed

Bob Baxter pleads his case, while manager Pat Daugherty steams.

while Baxter returned to the sidelines and warm-up again. The fans didn't seem to mind. A while later, with umpire Dave Steveley behind the plate, Baxter proceeded to retire the first nine hitters he faced and smiled his way to a complete-game, four-hit victory. A reporter for the *Post-Journal* newspaper asked what I thought about Baxter's performance. "I'd be willing to come here for the right price," I replied, "and give him a pep talk every time he pitches."

TWO: It's now 2003 and I walk into our Hollywood office to hear my co-host at the time, Dina Eastwood, say, "I've got a phone number for you." (I already had about nine different numbers for Dina and her husband Clint, and she had both of mine.) "Whose number?" I asked.

"It's Joe Torre's cell number. He wants you to call him."

"Yeah, right."

"Seriously, he was sitting next to me at a golf tournament and mentioned that you should pull a gag on the Yankees."

I was certain Dina had no idea I had approached the Yankees on several occasions about doing a sequence, and that the answer had always come back negative. I waited two weeks before calling the number, and the first thing I asked the Yankees manager was why now, after so many rejections? "You probably reached some of George's assistants," he said, referring to owner Steinbrenner. "I imagine they never asked him about it."

"And now George says it's okay?"

"I didn't say that. I just said we should do it."

A few weeks later the Yankees were scheduled to play a series in Anaheim where the Angels were all too happy to have me play some tricks—on the *Yankees*. I set myself up in an room near the Yankees clubhouse, pretending to be an executive from the office of the commissioner. Torre and his staff passed the word that a bigshot was hanging around and might want to talk privately with some players.

For first baseman Nick Johnson, a free-spirit type of guy, we designed a batting helmet with a satellite dish about the size of a cantaloupe mounted on top. I explained that TV viewers would get a great view of the action if certain players were actually transmitting video while playing. The helmet had various wires (which we borrowed from an EKG heart monitor) that snapped

**Nick Johnson
tightly wired.**

to adhesive pads on Nick's wrists and arms.

ME: Now just take your normal batting stance.

NICK: Shit! I can't be wearing this.

ME: The wires will be taped under your uniform.

NICK: I can't wear this. I've got too much shit on me!

ME: The fans will just love it, you know. You'll be like a miniature TV station out there on the field. What do you say, Nick? Will you give it a try?

NICK: Yeah, I'll give anything a try.

◆ ◆ ◆

THE HELMET ROUTINE was funny (note in the photo that we spared no expense: the "satellite transmitter" is made from a doorstop), but it was really just a safety gag in case my main plan for dealing with the Yankees players fell flat. It didn't.

Did you ever notice how professional baseball players spit a lot, especially during TV close-ups? I've never seen a professional basketball player spit on the court. Baseball players are unique in that they suffer from excessive saliva production. Then there's crotch-grabbing. If Major Leaguers aren't spitting they're rubbing their crotches.

When I confronted Yankees all-star catcher Jorge Posada with the spitting charge I thought he was going to faint. I told him the commissioner's office had monitored him spitting on television "847 times so far during the season." He professed to have no idea the totals were that high, but pledged to cut back. "I'm going to really watch for it now," he said.

Then I met with third baseman Robin Ventura, a savvy guy.

ROBIN: I think (spitting) is better than picking the nose. They're always getting a guy (on TV) and they're showing him in the dugout and he's picking his nose.

ME: The commissioner thinks we can do better...

I realized that Ventura had caught on and was toying with me. I introduced myself, and asked him not to spoil things because pitcher Andy Pettitte was on the way in, and there was reason to believe this would be our best take. The night before I had visited the Yankees broadcast booth to say hello to my friend Bobby Murcer, the former center fielder, whom I'd played with in golf tournaments and who was one of baseball's (many) nice guys. (Tragically, Bobby died five years later from a brain tumor.)

"You've got to get Andy Pettitte," he said without a beat. "We always joke about it in the booth; no one rubs his crotch on camera as much as Andy." Andy had a worried expression from the moment he walked in, and it only got worse as I told him he'd been caught too many times on *crotch-cam*.

ANDY: If I'm going to my crotch area, I don't know I'm going to my crotch area, or I'm adjusting my cup or something, you know?

ME: In other words, it's reflexive…

ANDY: Right.

ME: Would you say you're cognizant of making that move more this season than earlier in your career?

ANDY: You're kidding with me, right? This is a joke, right?

Andy gets a firm grip on the problem.

I told him it was "Candid Camera," and he was a good sport about the whole thing. Unlike Robin Ventura, Pettitte was totally caught in the gag—hook, line and jock strap.

The next day I was back at my office when Bill Cartwright called me into his editing room. "You've got to see this," he said. Bill began to run the tape of my conversation with Andy Pettitte. The video showed us sitting at a folding table, a bit larger than a card table, with Andy facing the camera. As he began to react to the crotch-rubbing problem, the camera pulls back to show under the table. The more Pettitte talked, the more he rubbed. We showed the piece twice on the air, the second time using slow-motion instant replay to highlight the, uh, action.

Three months after our shoot, Robin Ventura was traded to the Dodgers. Three months after it was televised, Nick Johnson was traded to the Expos. That same day Andy Pettitte left New York as a free agent and signed with the Astros. And a few years later Joe Torre became fed up and joined the Dodgers. Mere coincidence? Baseball historians will no doubt wrestle with it for years to come.

Personally, I just enjoy replaying the footage.

6 / A MILE HIGH

TO GIVE YOU AN IDEA of how eager my parents were to send me off to college, they got me into a school 1,731 miles away, bought me a midnight blue GTO, gave me an Amex card with my name on it, and ushered me out, at age 17, for a five-day solo drive across the country.

I had not been a particularly accomplished high school student, with my head in the clouds of Ditto fumes. The associate producer on "Candid Camera," Ann Richardson, who grew up in Colorado and was a University of Denver graduate, encouraged me to consider her alma mater. She mentioned several of the famous journalists who had attended DU, beginning with the legendary writer and broadcaster Lowell Thomas (class of 1912) who was a fixture for decades on radio and TV and delivered what is believed to be television's first news broadcast in 1930, as well as its first regularly scheduled newscast in 1940.

Someone of Thomas's stature should not be remembered for his on-air gaffes, but here is just one. He often delivered his nightly radio program from his home in Upstate New York and didn't always have time to review the script that was sent to him from Manhattan. One night the copy included the line, "She suffered a near-fatal heart attack," which, when Thomas read it for millions of listeners, became, "She suffered a near-fatal fart attack."

But I digress.

They hadn't invented GPS when I drove to Denver, so I obtained a AAA TripTik, often referred to by gas station attendants as a *map*. Remember maps? Fully spread out, one would cover the entire back seat, yet it never had quite enough detail to indicate how many miles before the next turn. Anyone able to properly refold one of these maps was destined to be good at solving a Rubik's Cube.

Mom also gave me a book of stamps in the denomination used for postcards. Before texting was invented, people on trips frequently wrote postcards with messages like:

> *"Arrived safely. Rain should let up by Friday. Here's a picture of the shop where I bought this postcard. Love, Pete."*

Dad gave me a roll of coins on the off-chance that I would find a working pay phone in, say, Terre Haute. He also loaned me a camera. Before cell phones, travelers actually carried cameras wherever they went, plus an enormous amount of what was known as *camera gear*—including rolls of film, a flash attachment, lenses, filters, tripod, and a ridiculously bulky case.

There were no ATMs back then, so getting cash was a major problem on trips if you didn't carry *travelers checks*. The most popular kind, issued by American Express, offered foolproof security by having you sign them in not one but *two* places. If you ran out of travelers checks you were forced to have money "wired" to you via Western Union, which had branches conveniently located in the seediest part of every town.

As I crossed the George Washington Bridge the first morning, I was terrified and clutched the wheel with both hands, at the exact "10 o'clock and 2 o'clock positions" that we learned in drivers' ed. (Remember, I was 17 and had only obtained my senior license a few months earlier.) By Ohio I confidently had my right hand on the wheel and my left arm out the window. In Nebraska, where I believe the speed limit was about 90, I began experimenting with, "How long can I go with *both* hands off the wheel?" And eventually, "How long can I go with both hands off the wheel and my eyes closed?"

As I zagged across America I encountered many informative road signs, such as LOW FLYING AIRCRAFT. (There's nothing in the drivers' manual about avoiding airplanes—which would have to be flying at about four-and-a-half feet to pose much of a threat.) On I-95 a sign said: "End Highway Safety Corridor." (Should drivers assume it's now OK to drive recklessly?) A few miles later: "DUI Enforcement Area." (Really? I assumed every foot of road in America is a DUI Enforcement Area.) On I-80: REST STOP. NO LOITERING. (Odd, because loitering is an integral part of the resting process.) Another

Interstate warning: FOG MAY BE ICY. (Is icy fog a solid, liquid or gas?)

After five days on the road I pulled my bug-covered GTO into a parking space at the University of Denver. It was a very scenic place that only smelled bad when the wind blew from the stockyards.

◆ ◆ ◆

DENVER WAS AN IDEAL WAY STATION on the path to growing up. For someone who had spent most of his time in semi-rural Croton, it was a large enough city, yet not threatening. It was like embarking on the highway of life—with

training wheels. Even beer was designed to give young adults an opportunity to gradually become comfortable with intoxication and throwing up in public.

Colorado had what was called 3.2 beer. For college students it was the equivalent of giving kids candy cigarettes, except that this drink had actual alcohol—3.2 percent as measured by weight. It was the only form of alcohol that 18-year-olds could legally consume in Colorado, and there were numerous clubs—"3.2 joints"—in downtown Denver that specialized in serving it. Every major brewery, including the local favorite Coors ("brewed with pure Rocky Mountain spring water"), produced 3.2 beer. The theory, dating back to the 1930s when President Franklin D. Roosevelt signed a law allowing this type of brew as a means of easing America out of prohibition, was that the alcohol level wasn't enough to make people drunk. Clearly, FDR had no way of knowing the extent to which DU students would dedicate themselves to disproving the theory. No matter how little alcohol a beverage has, if you manage to consume three pitchers of it you still wind up with a lot of alcohol in your system. (Plus, your chances of throwing up increase dramatically, which helps explain the distinctive odor in 3.2 joints.)

I had my fair share of low-alcohol beer, but managed to limit my experiences with pot, and I abstained entirely from the more mind-bending psychedelic drugs of the period. When tempted to try such chemicals, I'd remember watching my friend Steve, with his hair spray-painted green, running naked down the middle of Evans Boulevard. I was just too scared.

As with alcohol, Colorado was always fairly tolerant of drug use. In 2014 it became the first state to legalize retail marijuana sales for recreational use, which *The Denver Post* hailed as an "historistic swirl of commerce and cannabis."

DU's campus, five miles south of downtown Denver, looked like it had been created by architects who worked while stoned. There were modern buildings, like my ten-story dorm; stately old structures such as University Hall, built in 1890, and a raft of "temporary buildings" made of wood. By the time I took classes in these temps, freezing in winter and broiling in summer, they had been "scheduled for removal" for about three decades.

Several buildings at DU are named "Evans" in honor of John Evans, the territorial governor who founded the school in 1864. One year later, Evans was forced to resign because of his role in the Sand Creek Massacre—one of the worst slaughters of Native Americans in U.S. history. So, except for its first year, DU has had to deal with what historians refer to as a *checkered past*.

ALMOST EVERY MEMOIR that recounts college experiences mentions pizza, usually a lot of it. So, at least in that respect, my first semester at DU was normal. In addition to pizza I consumed enormous quantities of birthday cake, which I'll get to in a moment.

My roommate freshman year, who was definitely not named Maxwell Desmond III, came from a town on Long Island, N.Y. (I don't think I ever spoke with him long enough to find out exactly which one.) Before coming to DU we

had each filled out lengthy questionnaires covering things like academic interests, sleeping habits and sports preferences. Then some clerk must have said,
"These guys both live in the New York City suburbs," and placed us together,
failing to note that we had absolutely nothing else in common. Max was an oaf:
big, clumsy and clueless. He quickly established himself as the type of guy who
punched you in the shoulder to make a point, but too forcefully for what the
moment required. On the third day of our first semester Max went out after
dinner and returned about a month later to pick up his stuff. (He had dropped
out of school and was shacking up with a band until he ran out of money, at
which point the band members ran out of patience with having him around.)

In the evenings Canino's Pizzeria delivered roughly every 15 minutes.
The delivery guy was frequently stuck with unclaimed pizzas, so by stationing
ourselves in the lobby we could intercept the driver and offer him two bucks

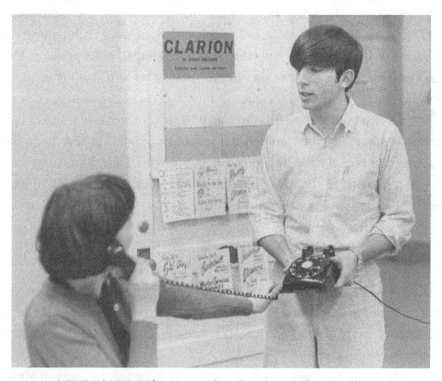

NEWS HOUND: When not eating pizza I wrote for the student
newspaper, *The Clarion*. Here, I'm flirting with Corky Deboer, our copy
editor, using the reliable "Let me hold that phone for you" come on.

for a large pie. As we got better at this, we realized that by phoning in fake orders there would be even more unclaimed two-dollar pizzas. On a typical day I would eat no breakfast, no lunch and then, between 4 p.m. and 2 a.m., maybe two or three sausage and onion pizzas.

A month after I arrived in Denver I decided to gift Mom on my 18th birthday by phoning home. "I wish you had a cake," she said sadly. I told her not to worry because I had plenty of pizza, but it got me thinking and thus was born "Birthday Cakes from Home," a business that made lots of money until I, literally, got sick of it.

I convinced a woman in DU's administrative office to help me with what I loosely described as "a research project," by lending me a copy of the thick document listing all of the roughly 5,000 undergrads along with their home addresses and dates of birth. From this I culled the names of freshmen and sophomores, and then hired students in my dorm to type mailing labels and stuff envelopes. Parents around the country were soon receiving letters that began:

School records indicate that your son or daughter's birthday is fast approaching. What better way to remind them how much they're missed, and how much you care, than with a personalized Birthday Cake from Home . . .

The key to this sales pitch was its opening reference to "school records," thereby signaling validation, if not actual participation, by the school. The letter went on to cajole the parents into making a purchase, with a price structure that took most of them right past the seven-inch cake with no inscription for $9.95, beyond the 12-inch "standard" cake with a small inscription at $14.95, and straight to the $29.95 "deluxe" cake that "most families tell us is the best way to show you care."

My small mailbox in the lobby of Centennial Towers—the kind with a little door that opens with a combination lock—could hold about ten letters. Soon I was getting as many as 15 a day. I made an deal with the Continental Baking Company, a large outfit that sold wholesale to stores and restaurants, to deliver each day's cake order directly to my dorm. Then, my helpers and I would head out to bring them to individual students on their birthdays. But as the semester progressed we found that more and more cakes were undeliverable. Seems that Max Desmond wasn't the only DU student to move without informing his parents of his whereabouts; each evening we'd be left with several undeliverable cakes.

At first my team used knives and forks, but before long we just grabbed fistfuls of cake with our hands, stuffed it in our mouths, and then threw the rest away. It was not a pretty sight, and after a few weeks was not a good feeling. I quit the birthday cake business near the end of freshman year.

◆ ◆ ◆

AS A JOURNALISM MAJOR, I wanted a part-time job in news. Imagine my glee upon seeing this posting on the Mass Communications bulletin board:

NEWS WRITER WANTED. NO EXPERIENCE NECESSARY.
WEEKEND SHIFT. KBTV, CHANNEL 9.

Had I not been so eager to apply I might have found time for skepticism about a "news writer" position for which experience was not a requisite—like hiring a barber who had never cut hair, or a mechanic who knew nothing about cars. The interview was conducted by a woman from the personnel department, who began by asking if I had ever noticed the Times Square-style news-ticker that ran around the top of a tall building on Broadway, about a mile south of KBTV's headquarters. I had. The TV station operated this ticker, and its headlines were written by the news staff. I had no experience; then again, how many resumes could she have received from news-ticker writers? She told me to report Saturday at 8 a.m.

When I arrived for work, I was shown equipment that Rube Goldberg would have admired. After typing headlines on ordinary paper, I'd have to retype everything, very, very slowly, on a special machine that punched round holes in inch-wide paper tape that unspooled from a large drum. Each hole represented a bulb on the sign. Letter by letter I'd create a pattern of punched holes until I had spelled out a full headline. The only way to fix a mistake was to either start over or cut the tape and glue in a replacement section—so it was wise to avoid mistakes. Once a batch of, say, a dozen headlines was completed, the tape was taken next door where it was wound into a continuous loop and fed through a gadget that "read" the holes as they passed a sensor. This sent signals a mile away to the sign where they were translated into a series of "on" and "off" cues for each bulb, making it seem as if the words I had written were "moving" around the top of the building. This entire process was repeated every two hours. I was now, for the first time in my life, a paid professional journalist with my work, if not my name, in lights.

I QUIT THE NEWS-TICKER BUSINESS the day word spread on campus that a big Hollywood production team was coming to Denver to shoot a movie called "The Protectors" and would be hiring locals as extras, stand-ins, doubles and a few bit players.

I don't recall whether I was first in line at the production trailer but I'm certain I was the most enthusiastic applicant. My pitch: I'll do anything. Work long hours? Yes! Skip classes to be on the set full-time for a month? OK! Shave my Beatles haircut to nearly a buzz cut? No problem! I was hired as a stand-in for the actor John Saxon, who a few years later would star opposite Bruce Lee in the martial arts classic "Enter the Dragon." John was one of the few cast members who appeared in enough scenes to guarantee that he and I would both work for 30 straight days. When it came time to meet the movie people, they were nothing like the college students and rock musicians with whom I'd been hanging. These folks from planet Hollywood all had beautiful skin, great hair, expensive-looking clothes—not just the actors but also the technicians and crew members.

It wasn't clear to me whether we would be shooting a theatrical film or a made-for-TV movie (it turned out to be both), but it was obvious that "The Protectors" was a B-level production, with a cast of has-beens and up-and-comers who shuttled in, shot a few quick scenes and then flew back to LA. The movie troupe reminded me of characters in the film "The Sting," those lovable con artists who gathered in Chicago, greeted one another with a wink and a tap on the nose, exchanged stories about their latest adventures, pulled a nice suit off the rack of clothes, did their jobs, were well paid, and left town in a hurry.

The call time on the first day of shooting was 5 p.m. on Larimer Street, in a renovated area downtown. The first order of business, announced at about 5:01, was "Lunch!" I soon realized that this group ate often and well, with carefully catered meals—referred to as "lunch" no matter what time they were served—delivered to wherever the crew happened to be.

A surreal aspect of the project was the fact that I never quite knew what "The Protectors" was about. Since I didn't merit a copy of the script, all I could piece together was that the plot involved assassins hired to rub out a wealthy businessman. Adding to my confusion was the fact that scenes were shot out of order, based solely upon availability of actors and locations. Also, I began to fear that the script wasn't very good. After paying close attention through the first week of filming I was certain of it.

As a stand-in, my job was to watch closely as John Saxon received his blocking instructions from the director, and then step in and repeat the required movements as many times as needed for the crew to set lights and position the camera. The primary female stand-in was a local girl, about my age, named Tia Tyler, who the year before had been Miss Denver and competed in the Miss America pageant, finishing in a three-way tie for the Miss Congeniality prize. Along with several crew members, I had an instant crush on her.

Although these Hollywood guys had good looks, plenty of money and a certain sophistication, I had something going for me in the competition for Tia's affection that they simply couldn't beat. She and I were required to stand together at close range for many hours each day, basically cooing at each other while the crew did its prep. (Sort of like the movie "Love Actually" but, regretfully, without the nudity.) And when our "work" was finished, we got to sit together for "Lunch!" After a few days, the assistant producer decided that Tia and I could handle all the stand-in work no matter which actors were in the scenes, which suited me just fine. I began to give serious consideration to pursuing a movie career.

I can't recall exactly how much I was paid as a stand-in, but I know it was plenty, and the producers kept offering me chances to make more. I parked my car in one shot and allowed it to be covered with fake snow, I was an extra in two scenes, and I doubled for John Saxon once by running across a parking lot, and with each of these little things came bonus money.

One night we filmed a scene in which the coroner was called after a shooting, and to my surprise he turned out to be the weatherman from Channel 2. He was among the lucky locals to be cast in small parts, and he delivered his lone line flawlessly: "I'd say it was a skull fracture and I'd say it produced an acute, massive subdural hemorrhage." In a small group of onlookers was a young skinny guy with long sideburns. My film debut.

By the time production ended I had gone on several dates with Tia and made more money than at any time in my life, except as a seller of birthday cakes.

When the film finally appeared on television the name had been changed from "The Protectors" to "Company of Killers." It also turned up in a few theaters and on home video with the title "The Hit Team." The critic in me is champing at the chance to lash out at the finished film, but I'm going to defer to Mr. D.B. Borroughs, of Glen Cove, New York, who has the distinction of being the lone person to post a review of "Company of Killers" on the Internet Movie Database:

> This is a very run of the mill TV movie that somehow got diverted to the big screen. ... I apologize for not being more detailed but while the movie wasn't bad it wasn't very good either, it just sort of lays there, not really a movie movie, and not really a TV movie. Watching this late last night I found myself slowly being put to sleep by it while at the same time trying to remain awake enough to find out what happened next (which does score points for it). Once it was over I moved on to other, more lively things.

And, as much as I loved being in the movie business, so did I.

7 / RADIO DAZE

ALTHOUGH MY FATHER AND I both wound up on television, we each got our start doing radio straight out of college. He created a syndicated radio show in the early forties called "The Funny Money Man," in which listeners participated by sending in trivial items for the chance to win trivial sums. ("We'll pay $1.35 to the first 12 people who send us a rusty paperclip.") It was hardly a ratings smash but it proved two points: (1) Folks are easily swept up in the concept of winning something rather than focusing on how much they've won, (2) For many of us, a penny at the gas pump has vivid significance but billions of dollars create a meaningless blur. We are unable to fathom the big numbers in our modern world, a condition known as *innumeracy*. Government and business spend billions here, billions there and, as the late Sen. Everett Dirksen famously concluded, "pretty soon you're talking about real money."

I didn't give much thought to working in radio until I arrived at DU, where the student-run station called itself KVDU, "broadcasting" for a distance of about 40 feet to a single speaker in the next room. Several of us developed a plan to move KVDU out of the Mass Comm Department and make it a stand-alone student-run property. We persuaded the school to give us our own building—a dilapidated wooden house, actually—on nearby York Street. They said if we could fix it up and maintain it, the place was ours. It consisted of a living room, two bedrooms, plus a kitchen and bathroom. Besides being old, it was made entirely of wood—a creaky, non-soundproof structure that was just about the worst possible place to do radio. But there were no meddling faculty members around, in fact no one over age 20, and we had the keys.

Everyone in radio back then used a fake name, so on KVDU I called myself Deke Jason ("This is your DJ, DJ." I thought I was soooo damn clever.) Local professionals with their own fake names occasionally dropped by to check us out, among them Jay Alexander, 30ish and rotund. When he started doing news on KBTR he called himself Jay Van Alexander, then one day he decided— or more likely was told by his boss—to drop "Van" and go with Jay Alexander. A few weeks later the "Jay" was gone and he had become Van Alexander. Some afternoons he'd pull up to our building on York Street in the KBTR mobile cruiser and ask if any of us wanted a ride. Funny about that: just a year earlier we would have killed for a chance to ride around in that hot vehicle with its important-looking antennae poking up from the roof and the big, bright letters KBTR on the sides. But now we were so successful in our own world, so into ourselves, that few of us ever went with Jay on his joy rides.

Dave Capps was another. On KBTR he had the midnight-to-six a.m. DJ shift, which in those days was a live, remote broadcast from the Celebrity Lanes bowling alley on Colorado Boulevard. Dave borrowed his on-air name from the great Green Bay Packers quarterback and spelled it the same way. Next to his little perch at the bowling alley's front desk was a sign that said: LIVE! ALL NIGHT! KBTR's BART STARR! Since we college students didn't spend a lot of time sleeping, at least at night, we'd often visit Dave and watch him do his show, which was a gloomy experience because there just weren't many folks bowling at 4 a.m. Dave was a super nice guy, but he had the poor judgment to refer to himself on the air as "Captain Bart," and between records he played sound effects of boat whistles, which made listeners think he was an old-timer rather than someone yet to reach 25. His show was an annoying combination of foghorns and rock music, interrupted every few minutes by the smashing of bowling pins. Yet, Dave was our idol. My friends and I, immersed in learning about radio at KVDU, never lost sight of the fact that Dave drove a Jaguar XKE and was a big-time DJ in the nation's twentieth largest market.

◆ ◆ ◆

SOPHOMORE YEAR I hosted a talk program called "The Hellbox." Sounds daring but it's actually an old newspaper term. In composing rooms, broken pieces of lead type were tossed into a wooden container known as a "hellbox," where they'd sit until melted down and made into new type. I loved the notion

I hosted "The Hellbox" on KVDU. Here, I'm flirting with Miss Denver,
Holly Smith, using the reliable "Would you like to be on the radio?" come on.

that randomly sitting in the box these letters might form a word or phrase,
just as I hoped meaning would emerge magically from the ideas blurted on my
radio show. The program covered a wide range of topics: one night the guest
was a local beauty queen named Holly Smith, regaling listeners about bath-
ing-suit competitions; the very next show featured my exclusive interview
with Dr. Martin Luther King Jr. on the subject of race relations. Dr. King had
delivered a speech at DU that evening, and afterward students gathered in the
middle of campus and burned a junker car with a cross attached to the roof.
When police arrived the students avoided arrest by chanting "Higher pay for
cops!" As my interview began there were sirens in the background and considerable hubbub, yet Dr. King didn't seem to be the slightest bit concerned.

Another "Hellbox" guest was the football player O. J. Simpson. Back then,
long before his personal and legal problems revealed what must have been
inherent emotional imbalance, he spoke eloquently about his childhood in
San Francisco. As a child, Simpson had a medical condition that required him
to wear braces on both legs, yet he went on to become a star football player
in high school and, at the time of my interview, he had just led the nation in

rushing yards at USC. Sad, really, that his message to "Hellbox" listeners was to stay in school and make the most of their God-given abilities—a gospel O. J. was unable to follow himself.

One chilly Saturday night, a bunch of us became bored with what we were doing at KVDU and phoned the all-night DJ at KBTR, using the secret hotline number I had learned while working at Channel 9. We knew that after midnight he would be alone playing records, while literally locked into the building at the Mullins Broadcasting Company. I claimed to be a staff news-man, calling from the scene of a fire at Colorado Women's College. The jock immediately stopped the music and put me on for a live report. I tried to down-play the fire part and refrained from saying anything about injuries; my focus was on "dozens of naked girls, forced from their dormitory and now scamper-ing nude in the street!" I told the DJ I would gather more information and call back, which I did—three times. In each report the naked girls got more atten-tion: some were "frolicking," while others were "cavorting" as "crowds formed to get a look." What I didn't realize until much later was that as a result of my reports crowds were, indeed, forming. I was also unaware that Denver police had to break down the door at the station to halt the false broadcasts.

The whole thing was quite a hoot for everyone at KVDU until we read in *The Denver Post* two days later that the FBI had been called in to investigate. I'm able to chuckle about it now, believing as I do that the statute of limita-tions has expired.

A PREMATURELY BALDING, frumpy looking guy named Barry Fey showed up at KVDU one day to promote a concert at the DU student union featuring one of the hottest groups of the period, The Association. This six-member band would eventually sell over 80 million records with songs like "Along Comes Mary" and the follow-up hits "Cherish" and "Windy." We happily ran Fey's commercials and held contests for free passes, and the concert's 2,500 tickets quickly sold out. I don't know to what extent Fey believed I was personally responsible for his success at DU, but a short time later he offered me a job doing public relations for a music venue he was opening on West Evans Avenue. I never cared much for the PR side of media, and to this day I consider it journalism's evil twin, but this offer was just too good to turn down.

Fey had endured a messed-up childhood—born in New York where he lost his father at an early age, moving to Chicago and falling in with violent street gangs, then enlisting in the Marines while weighing 237 pounds. After

The Dog's posters often played tricks. This one is for Chuck Berry.

the Marines he tried college for a while (some people have all the luck: DU assigned me Max Desmond as a roommate, while the University of Pennsylvania randomly gave Fey the future talk-show host Maury Povich). But Fey dropped out after little more than a year, found work at a Chicago racetrack, and then moved to Denver where he began promoting college concerts.

Fey saw an ad in Billboard magazine seeking bands to play in San Francisco so he rushed out there to pitch a Colorado group called Eighth Penny Matter. That's how he met Chet Helms, a one-time partner with Bill Graham in the legendary Fillmore Auditorium

and then operator of the Avalon Ballroom, known worldwide as the crucible of San Francisco's distinctive rock sound. Helms wasn't particularly interested in the band Fey was promoting, but agreed to back Fey in a Denver start-up: a club to bear the name of the production company Helms operated in San Francisco, The Family Dog. This was the new venture Barry Fey wanted me to help publicize.

Even if you've never heard of Fey, Helms or The Family Dog, you'd immediately recognize the posters—psychedelic masterpieces created in San Francisco by the top graphic designers of the day. And even if you weren't familiar with the posters, you couldn't possibly fail to recognize the featured acts we had—for instance, in just the first month: Janis Joplin with Big Brother & The Holding Company . . . the Grateful Dead . . . Captain Beefheart . . . The Doors. Soon after that: Buffalo Springfield . . . Van Morrison . . . Jefferson Airplane. My job was to distribute flyers and create commercials to be played on KVDU. For this I was not only paid money, I was also allowed to attend the shows and hang near, although not exactly *with,* those incredible musicians.

The Family Dog was a cavernous place with a balcony in which affluent customers could sit in chairs and order drinks. Everyone else sprawled on the floor below. There was elaborate lighting by a company Helms also owned called Dioginese Lantern Works. The air was so thick with pot smoke that you got a contact high within minutes. The Dog closed after a few months because the owners cared more about music than paying rent.

◆ ◆ ◆

ONE EVENING IN 1968 I got a call from Russ Dobson, a friend at DU, who said in his deep, melodious radio voice, that he was quitting his weekend news job at KMYR-FM. The job required a Third Class FCC license, or "ticket" as it is called. First Class tickets, issued to people with actual knowledge of technical transmission procedures, demand considerable studying. Third class tickets, however, are more like library cards—you can get one pretty much by asking, and once licensed are authorized to check various dials and meters on a station's equipment and record the data.

As part of my audition at KMYR I read a bit of copy and a station promo. The program director's quick decision to offer me the job seemed less related to my audition than to three other factors: (1) I had my Third Class ticket, (2) Russ was leaving on Saturday, and (3) it was already Thursday afternoon. Russ spent the remainder of Thursday training me and saying goodbye. It was the last time I saw him—or, for that matter, any other living person at KMYR.

KMYR was a fully automated station, which, in pre-computer days, was a strange and unwieldy arrangement. Music was played on oversized reel-to-reel machines; the "hosts," also on tape, worked for a national service based in Los Angeles; local commercials and station promos were played on cart machines. All of these devices were switched on and off by a master time clock—the type of thing you might use to control sprinklers on your lawn. And the hourly newscasts? They had to be pre-recorded on five-minute carts and placed in the machine in time to be started automatically, precisely on the hour. Finished or not, they were cut off five minutes later.

I'd arrive at 8 a.m. Saturday and let myself in . . . check that the tele-type machine hadn't jammed overnight . . . write transmitter readings in the log book (I had absolutely no idea how to do this, so for all my time at KMYR I copied numbers from the previous day's entries) . . . write and record hourly newscasts. I was also responsible for answering the phone, but as best as I can remember no one ever called. I'd lock up at 5:05 p.m. Saturday, marking the end of the station's news coverage for the day, and then return on Sunday to repeat the process.

Among the first lessons I learned is that it can be more difficult to pre-record a newscast than to do it live. Many broadcasters experience this—in part because the pressure is missing. Conservative blowhard Bill O'Reilly had a memorable meltdown pre-taping a short closing for the syndicated pro-gram "Inside Edition":

...That's tomorrow, and that is it for us today (cut) ...That's tomor-row (cut) ... That's tomorrow and that (cut) ...That's tomorrow and that is it for us today and (cut)—I can't do it, (screaming) I can't do it, we'll do it live. We'll do it live. F--- it! We'll do it live! I'll write it and we'll do it live! This f---ing thing sucks!

Unlike O'Reilly's fiasco, my foul-ups while pre-recording the news are, mercifully, not preserved for eternity on YouTube.

I was in a windowless office, so isolated that if something major had ever happened right outside the building I probably wouldn't have known about it until reading the next day's *Denver Post*. During my five months at

KMYR I don't recall anyone ever saying that they heard me on the radio. The result was sort of a tree-falling-in-the-forest sensation. If I was broadcasting but no one ever heard me, was I making any noise?

◆ ◆ ◆

EVERYTHING CHANGED the day I walked into the Petroleum Club Building at 16th and Broadway for my first day as weekend newscaster at KHOW Radio. This AM station had real, living people behind the microphones 24/7 and was top-rated, with a competitive news department.

My shift was 9 a.m. to 6 p.m. on Saturdays and Sundays. However, with no unions to set limits, KHOW's news team was expected to be on call 24/7. Each newsman was given an expensive two-way radio for his private car as well as a "personal unit"—worn in an official-looking shoulder holster, with "KHOW" printed on the sides. There were no cell phones in this era, so the idea that any one of us could be standing at, say, the supermarket checkout counter and receive a "call" on our personal unit to respond to a fire or robbery was impressive. "He's from K-HOW," people would whisper in apparent awe as we dropped our groceries and rushed out the door.

Bob Scott, the news director, had rigid rules for the two-way system. For instance, we were not allowed to use our names; we referred to each other only by number. I was "Car 2," while Bob was "Car 6," and when we were out of our cars using our personal units, we became "X-2" and "X-6." We were required to contact the newsroom whenever we left home ("Car 2 is in the car, heading north on University Boulevard") and to report whenever we got out of the car ("X-2, out at the dry cleaners"). At the end of each day we were "out at home," recharging our batteries—literally and figuratively—and reachable by telephone.

Broadcast news coverage in small- and medium-sized markets back then, and to a great extent to this day, focused on four major themes: traffic, weather, police and fire. Without large reporting staffs it was impossible to cover more complex stories that demanded research and multiple interviews and could take up an entire day to assemble. So local radio gravitated to what it could do best: respond quickly to emergency developments, a process that came to be known derisively as "ambulance chasing."

At KHOW, we not only chased ambulances—as well as police cars and fire trucks—we frequently beat them to their destinations. If the police radio announced a "10-50 (auto accident) with injuries," and one of us was in the vicinity, we'd hit the gas and often arrive before the cops. It was extraordinarily dangerous since none of our cars had flashing lights, yet we answered these calls at high rates of speed and violated most traffic regulations en route. This was part of a tacit agreement by which we would never question or criticize the work of police and fire officials on the air and they, in return, would wink at our reckless driving.

One afternoon I was leaving class at DU when the radio said there had been a multi-vehicle crash on I-25. I jumped in my car and sped south at about 90 mph, arriving just after two fire trucks, but before any cleanup took place. I parked on the grass in the center median, leaped out with my personal X unit, and informed the newsroom I was ready to go live. This was also typical—we'd often report first and ask the necessary questions later. Soon I was telling KHOW listeners:

I've just arrived at the scene of a serious crash with fatalities on the northbound side of I-25, about 20 miles south of the city. Fire personnel are assisting victims, and traffic is stopped in both directions. As I walk onto the highway now, I can see wreckage strewn about from what must have been a violent crash involving two cars. I see a shoe . . . a hat . . . some papers . . . and what looks like steaks for a family picnic of some kind. We'll be back with more after we speak with police. . .

While finishing my report I had moved toward the fire captain. "Son," he said after I had signed off, "there's no picnic. What you saw on the pavement was, I believe, part of the driver's arm."

I thought I was going to throw up on the captain's feet. I turned and went back to my car, trying to refocus. I heard the station calling on the speaker under my dashboard, but for a few moments I couldn't talk. I finally composed myself, and a few minutes later Bob Scott roared in to take over the coverage. I drove back to DU in the far right lane, at about 45 mph. To this day I wince when I hear of journalists speeding to cover stories, or see TV reporters needlessly bobbing around in the path of hurricanes.

◆ ◆ ◆

TOWARD THE END of my senior year, Bob Scott gave me my first full time job, doing newscasts on KHOW between 10 a.m. and 2 p.m., Monday to Friday. That didn't allow much time for classes at DU, but I was doing much better in college than I had in high school—managing to never take French or any other foreign language.

One Tuesday, I was writing the one o'clock newscast when something in the first story, about banks and a bank official named Shanks, made me chuckle and begin to fiddle with the words. Without giving it much thought I proceeded to write the entire newscast in rhyme.

> *It's news time, folks, if you please,*
> *Denver temperature, 40 degrees.*

Then I did the banking story featuring Mr. Shanks, and continued my tortured rhymes for every line of the five-minute newscast. I ended with:

> *There you have it,*
> *My midday views;*
> *This is Funt,*
> *K-HOW 60-30 News!*

When it was over I believed I had accomplished some remarkable feat—something so engaging that Bob would probably insist that I make it a regular feature. That didn't happen. In fact no one said much of anything, the way people act when you have a mustard stain on your tie and they politely choose not to mention it. Later, I asked Bob if he had happened to catch the one o'clock news. "Yup."

"Well, what did you think?"

"I think you're a talented young man, who probably doesn't understand how hard some of us have worked to get where we are in this business, and how desperately we want to hold on to our jobs."

I didn't say anything more, and I never tried rhyming a newscast again. I do note for the record that years later one of broadcasting's most accomplished journalists, Charles Osgood, built a name for himself by rhyming the news on CBS Radio. He even wrote a book about his unique approach called, "Nothing Could Be Finer Than a Crisis That Is Minor in the Morning." Still, listeners are more inclined to accept rhymes from a veteran like Osgood than from a 20-year-old who, if he spent more time in class, might know better.

The morning hosts at KHOW were "Buzz and Barney." Buzz Lawrence got his start nearly 30 years earlier as a Dixieland pianist on the "Major Bowes Amateur Hour" program; Rosemary Barnwell was the 1966 Miss Colorado Universe. I'd be starting my news shift just as "Buzz and Barney" was winding down. Despite their early hours they always looked like a couple on a date, dressed as if heading out to dinner—in fact, following their show they almost always attended station functions and sales events. Buzz treated his 22-year-old partner like a trinket. As a couple they were in demand for supermarket openings, award ceremonies and various KHOW promotions.

Colorado is known for growing wheat, but in my experience its best crop was beauty queens. I had tried to date Holly Smith at DU, had quite a thing going with Tia Tyler while shooting the movie, and now Rosemary Barnwell was on the other side of the large glass window that separated the newsroom from the production studio. One morning as I finished my 10 a.m. newscast, she and Buzz stepped into the production studio to record commercials. Without thinking, and remarkably out of character, I scribbled a note with a red grease pencil on a sheet of copy paper: *Dinner tonight?* When Buzz turned his back, I pressed the note against the glass.

What could have been one of the most embarrassing moments of my life became one of the best when Rosemary smiled and nodded yes. She didn't even seem to have to think about it.

At dinner I felt important yet extraordinarily nervous. Rosemary was a big Denver personality; she was worldly and socially skilled. The Miss Colorado pageant and national Miss USA competition gave her maturity and poise, while hundreds of lunches and dinners with drunken radio executives and sales people made her wise beyond her years. And me? Well, in four years at DU I hadn't ever eaten in a fancy restaurant, so this date was quite a special occasion.

Before long Rosemary and I were inseparable. The closer we became the more it irked management. She was one of the station's most valuable assets: her face was in newspaper ads and on billboards around town, and the public's perception—at least as Buzz understood it—was that "Buzz and Barney" were somehow linked as a couple. The staff began to act as if I was breaking up a marriage. Even her brother Jay, a pilot who frequently did the "Sky Spy" traffic reports, seemed to think his sister and I were messing up a good thing.

Then one night we messed it up for good.

We knew of a large billboard on a highway west of the city promoting KHOW's top performers. In the lower right corner it said: BOB SCOTT FRESH NEWS! For reasons that must have made sense at the time, I decided that Roe and I should paint over Bob's name and replace it with BARRY WIDOM— the station's police-schmoozing reporter whose name the public rarely ever heard.

At about midnight we pulled off the highway in the forest green Mercury Cougar I was now driving, and bounced along the dirt service road until we reached the sign. Naturally, it was bigger and higher off the ground than we had imagined. I pulled under the sign and climbed onto the roof with paint and brushes. The sign was illuminated in such a way that to motorists on the highway the two of us must have looked like circus performers in the spotlight of the center ring.

The following day word gradually spread at KHOW about the defaced billboard. Some thought it was funny, some didn't care, but everyone was wildly curious about who would do such a thing. Unable to pass up the credit we deserved, we began to boast about our little prank.

A few days later Rosemary was fired.

I was given a lecture by Bob Scott and was allowed to stay. I took a week's vacation and Roe and I flew back East to visit my family in Croton.

When I returned to Denver I was demoted from my air shift and offered a job as full-time street reporter, which I declined.

(Some months later Rosemary was rehired at KHOW and teamed with Buzz Lawrence's successor, Charlie Martin, for the highly successful "Charlie and Barney" program.)

As I removed the Family Dog posters from the wall of my apartment and packed the rest of my stuff, I computed that in four years I had worked at a dozen different jobs in Denver. I also had a journalism degree and a better outlook on life.

With my Cougar's radio pounding out hit songs, I pulled onto the highway for the drive back to New York. As has always been my nature, I was doing a running commentary, sort of a play-by-play of my life:

And so, with the majestic, snow-covered mountains rising before me, I accelerate and begin the long journey ...

I actually said those words aloud. Until I realized that the mountains are *west* of Denver, and I was heading in the wrong direction. I turned around at the next exit and, with less ceremony, headed home.

8 / FOODIE

HERE IS ONE of my favorite food sequences from "Candid Camera." See if you can guess the gag:

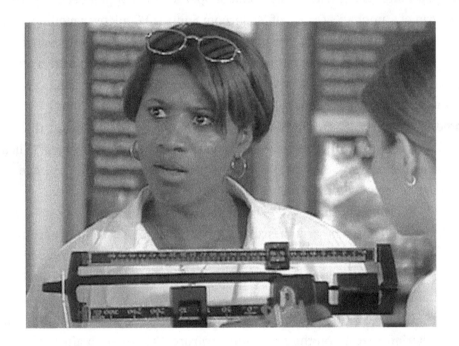

The woman had just arrived at a restaurant and was informed of a new policy: We weigh you first, and after you eat we weigh you again. Your bill is based on how much weight you gain. I love her expression. It captures the absurdity of the situation and the customer's predicament.

One guy asked, "Will I be allowed to use the bathroom before being weighed the second time?"

♦ ♦ ♦

MY FAVORITE MEAL IS CAESAR SALAD (no anchovies) piled on top of plain spaghetti (no sauce of any kind). I also like tuna fish on plain spaghetti or veggie hotdogs sliced on top of plain spaghetti with a squirt of ketchup. My wife Amy, who is an excellent cook, has informed me, "You have a very limited palate."

Soon after we met I cooked dinner for Amy using the recipe my father taught me—the only one he ever knew. (a) Place cut up pieces of beef or poultry in a skillet along with sliced green pepper and a chopped pear. (b) Stir in one can of Campbell's Cream of Mushroom Soup. (c) Cook over medium heat. (d) Serve over rice (although plain spaghetti is also a pleasant alternative).

Sheltered as I was during my youth, I never tasted pizza until I went to college, which explains why it was the only thing I ate during my first semester other than birthday cake. I never had Chinese food until I graduated from college and went to work at ABC News, which is why for the first six months there I ordered delivery of chicken lo mein every evening. (These experiences might also explain why I was only in my thirties when I had my gallbladder removed.)

I've since studied how to eat responsibly. For instance, I learned that nuts are good for your cardiovascular system because they contain unsaturated fatty acids. I enjoy eating them with raisins in trail mix and discovered that if you buy the kind with enough M&Ms you barely taste the nuts and raisins. It's almost like eating candy.

I read that breakfast is the most important meal of the day. According to Catherine Saxelby on the *Foodwatch* website: "There are oodles of breakfast cereals. What I want is one with the most fiber and/or whole grains but the lowest sugars and sodium." Thing is, the cereals Ms. Saxelby favors are painfully bland. My trick is to add oodles of maple syrup, because almost anything healthy tastes better with maple syrup.

Cooking Light magazine informed me that "Popcorn has a lot of bulk for its calories so it helps fill you up." They suggest three and a half cups of fat-free popcorn made in a microwave. However, I feel even more filled up after eating an entire bag from Trader Joe's—preferably the kettle-corn variety.

Many "health nuts" swear by hummus, that Middle Eastern mush of chickpeas, tahini and other flavorings. I've incorporated hummus into my diet by combining it with a large bag of "scoop-style" potato chips and a significant quantity of beer. (I always choose a "light beer" to avoid "empty calories.")

I've never been a fan of plain yogurt, even drowned in maple syrup. Yet, science tells us this B12-rich food works wonders, such as reducing moodiness. So I'd like to give a shout out to the Yoplait company for thoroughly de-yogurtizing yogurt. Among Yoplait's best flavors are Strawberry Cheesecake and Boston Cream Pie. I'll bet Yoplait doesn't even realize that health-conscious kids are drawn to the photos of cake and pie on the containers. Yoplait teamed with Dunkin' Donuts to create "Apple Fritter," described on its website as, "Beloved bakery pastry turned yogurt, this variety offers warm apple notes and delicious glazed donut flavors." (I wonder what level of sugar high is required to write ad copy about "warm apple notes"?)

Speaking of fruit, apparently I wasn't consuming enough of it, so I joined the civilized world by purchasing a juice-making machine. Here's a recipe I created. (a) Liquefy fruit. (b) Mix one part juice with two parts vodka. (c) Serve with or without ice (with or without the juice).

I struggled with diet and nutrition until I read this helpful advice from *WebMD*: "If you eat a high-calorie food or meal, balance your intake by choosing low-calorie foods the rest of the day or the next day." This simple tip has pretty much changed my life. Now I can eat a large pizza with three toppings from Domino's in the evening while watching a ballgame, knowing that although it's "high-calorie" I'll balance it with something low-calorie, like popcorn, in the remaining hour before bed.

I never lose sight of the fact that all consumption is healthy if it takes place outside the home—at a party, a restaurant, sports stadium, etc. These are locations where experts advise, "be good to yourself." Another thing: *Free* food never counts against a diet, nor does birthday cake, nor Buffalo wings at an all-you-can-eat buffet.

◆ ◆ ◆

HERE'S ANOTHER FAVORITE FOOD GAG: This man is standing six feet from the hostess in a restaurant that has plenty of empty tables. On entering he was told, "We require reservations." So he's using a phone to make a reservation by speaking to that same hostess—whose back is now turned as she pretends to be unaware that he's close by.

"What time will you be arriving?" she asks. And: "Do you need driving directions?"

One guy put down the phone and tapped the hostess on her shoulder, hoping to halt the insanity.

"Just a minute," she said. "I'm on the phone."

I LEARNED from observing my father that the one type of cooking men are required to pretend to master is barbecuing—a rich tradition that has served everyone from Ben Franklin to Clark Griswold. Dad spent so much time trying to get charcoal to burn properly that he had little time or patience for actual cooking. His trick was to encourage oil and grease to fall into the coals, causing a flare-up that would set the food on fire. As soon as the outside of whatever he was cooking was blackened, he pronounced it done.

Having watched years of this (while eating charred meat that was raw inside), I've tried to do better. I bought a wimpy Weber gas grill that comes with an electric lighter. I also acquired a Grillbot—battery-powered, with rotating wire brushes—that bangs around inside the Weber until most of the "visible" dirt is scraped away. Funny thing about me and dirt: Inside our house I'm germaphobic, frantic about any speck of dirt on or near my food; outside I'm like, "Dirt adds flavor. Besides, it can't hurt you once it's blasted by the flames." Recently, I discovered a surefire grilling method: Cook the food in a microwave before placing it on the grill. As soon as you sear in those nice black grilling marks, it's ready to serve, with a side of spaghetti.

IN DECADES OF DOING "CANDID CAMERA" shows, gags about food and dining have always been popular. Acknowledging that, when Dad died in 1999 we held his memorial at Mel's Diner in Hollywood. In my remarks I noted that, "Mel's hasn't had a funeral since it stopped serving the liver and onions," a quip that was greeted with appreciative chuckles from the kitchen staff.

Dad once rigged a diner stool so it sank lower as the customer ate. He cut spoons in half and then glued them back together with stuff that melted when placed in hot coffee, leaving people holding half a spoon. He had a staff member dunk his doughnut in strangers' coffee. A favorite prop was a "Squirting Grapefruit" that shot a stream of juice at people sitting nearby.

I did a lunch-counter routine in which I sat next to unsuspecting people and when they ordered I casually said, "I'll have the same." By prearrangement, the kitchen sent out a humongous portion for me, and barely anything for the other folks. I once played a waiter, explaining that everything was extra: Sugar packets, 10 cents; Ketchup packets, a nickel, etc. Another time I wrote a 2,000-word list of "daily specials" so our waitress could start reading them to customers . . . and never finish.

ONE MORE FAVE: In Los Angeles the city rates restaurants from "A" to "F," with "A" being the best ranking.

When this woman placed her order the grade posted behind her was "A." But as she waited for her food to arrive, a guy from the health department changed the grade to "F."

In this photo she is contemplating her first bite of food. Do I walk out? Do I dare eat my meal in an F-rated restaurant?

A CULINARY COLLEGE in Connecticut once allowed me to pretend to be the instructor when students arrived for their first class. Dressed beautifully (I must say), in a white chef's outfit with one of those tall toque hats, I informed the class that the two most important things for them to master in the kitchen are: (1) describing foods using a fake foreign accent, preferably French, and (2) the ability to decorate fruits and vegetables with useless embellishments.

We spent the next half-hour carving faces in cucumbers.

9 / BIG CITY SCALLYWAG

EVEN AS A MINOR FIGURE in Denver's media mix I felt important—not a star by any means, but a real player. I anchored the news five times a day on one of the market's top stations and thousands of people, some of whom were not stoned, heard what I had to say. Now, walking the streets of mid-Manhattan looking for my next job I felt invisible.

I auditioned for a job as a substitute newscaster at WINS, the all-news radio station. I was handed a roll of seemingly endless wire service reports, about the size of a roll of paper towels, and told to prepare a five-minute news-cast. I struggled but came up with the best script I could, and then was escort-ed to a small announcing booth where, with an engineer at the controls—a setup I had never seen before—I recorded my newscast.

I waited a few minutes before learning from a courteous young wom-an, who I believe was an assistant to someone's assistant, that I would not be working at WINS.

My next stop was on Sixth Avenue at 53rd Street, at the home of the greatest rock 'n roll station of all time. I had grown up listening to WABC, as did everyone I knew. The DJs–Big Dan Ingram, "Cousin Brucie" Morrow and the rest–were people I carried with me on a transistor radio throughout high school, from the moment I woke up until I fell asleep with the radio next to my ear. Riding the elevator to WABC's eighth floor headquarters was like making the initial ascent on a roller coaster, when your heart pounds as you rise and you think furiously about what it will be like at the top.

I got the job at WABC: a vacation-relief news writer position that only guaranteed four months employment, switching shifts every two weeks to cover for whoever was away.

My parents, after 18 years of marriage and dull suburban life, were divorced and living in separate apartments in Manhattan, and I was staying in the spare bedroom at my Mom's place on East 77th Street. As I got dressed for my first day of work at WABC I listened to Harry Harrison's morning show. In less than an hour I'd be able to connect faces with the familiar voices, and my mind was racing. Should I call him Mr. Harrison? What about Dan Ingram . . . did co-workers call him Big Dan? What did the newsroom look like? I took the bus down Fifth Avenue, walked a block over to Sixth Avenue, and then floated in the elevator to the eighth floor.

I didn't recognize him at the time, but the man standing next to me in the elevator with curly black hair and glasses was Rick Sklar, the nation's most influential rock-radio executive. In six years as WABC's program director he had elevated the station to number one in New York and made it the most listened-to radio station of all time. He favored DJs who appealed to the entire family . . . used a very short playlist of songs . . . relied on heavy promotion (when the Beatles burst onto the scene he renamed the station W-A-Beatle-C). On my second day I worked a shift that began at 6 a.m. At about 8 o'clock the editor casually suggested that, as the junior guy on duty, I could "have the pleasure of waking up the Coach."

Howard Cosell was a true legend—among colleagues, listeners, and in his own mind. He was eccentric, egocentric, wore a bad toupee (are there any good ones?) and smoked nasty smelling cigars. He was also one of the most talented broadcasters who ever lived.

Even before the launch of "Monday Night Football," which would happen in September of 1970, Cosell had as hectic a schedule as any broadcaster. At 8 most mornings he would be asleep at his house in Pound Ridge, N.Y., or his apartment on Manhattan's East Side. Both locations had broadcast lines installed so he could deliver radio sportscasts directly from home while still in his pajamas. So, at 8:05 I dialed Cosell's private number and heard the voice that *The New York Times* once described as, "a clutched-throat, high-pitched Brooklyn twang with a stately staccato that tended to put equal stress on each syllable of every word, infusing even the most mundane event with high drama." That's exactly what it sounded like over the phone when the Coach said, "Yes, yes. I'm up!"

Without pleasantries he asked for the overnight sports scores. Reading from wire copy I told him: "White Sox 4, Orioles 2 . . . Yanks 6, Red Sox 5, in 11 innings . . . the Yankees traded Dave McDonald to the Expos for Gary Waslewski . . ." I assume Howard was writing all this down, although I never asked. I stayed on the line briefly while he collected his thoughts, and then I hung up. At exactly 8:25 a.m., the speaker in the newsroom blared: "Hello again everyone, Howard Cosell, 'Speaking of Sports,' for American Contemporary Radio . . ." What followed was an ad-libbed, flawlessly delivered sports report and commentary.

Many of us can "fill" five minutes on radio or ad-lib a story. What Cosell did in his thrice-daily reports was different—he spoke extemporaneously while making it seem that he was reading a script. That's the exact opposite of what most broadcasters try to achieve.

Mocking Cosell and trying to ignite his temper was a competitive sport among WABC's staff whenever the Coach showed up in the building. The best prank occurred one Friday afternoon as Howard taped his Sunday interview show, known as "Speaking of Everything." The guest was Pete Axthelm, the renowned *Sports Illustrated* columnist. On cue, the Coach boomed, "Hello again everyone. Howard Cosell for American Contemporary Radio . . ." and the director's voice from the control room said stop. He explained that there was a *buzzing* sound. "Let's try it again."

"Hello again everyone, Howard Cosell . . ."

"I'm sorry Howard. We're still hearing that buzz."

The Coach boiled over. "It's a simple radio show!" he thundered, "It ain't a one-hour television spectacular." This went on for several minutes. Howard offered to share a mic with Axthelm . . . he recited a list of shows he still had to do that day on both radio and TV, exclaiming at one point, "I'm going nuts with all these shows!"

Finally, Cosell told his guest: "There's a time when even the greatest professional breaks down."

It's unclear how much, if any, buzz there was. The technicians were amusing themselves at Howard's expense.

Dan Ingram maintained a collection of tapes that included Cosell's funniest moments, as well as his own. One of the best occurred as Dan read a weather report predicting "brief showers." Just then Cousin Brucie stepped into Studio 8A and tossed a dozen Jockey briefs at Dan, who cracked up for almost a full minute. Dan informed listeners about the undershorts, noting, "They *smell* new."

◆ ◆ ◆

MUCH AS I LIKED working among these characters, it was a treat to get out to cover stories—such as the Beatles concert at Shea Stadium. I wonder what my answer would have been had my boss asked, "How much would you be willing to pay me for the Shea Stadium assignment?" Answer: a lot.

Then again, I probably would have paid plenty to *not* cover racial disturbances in Asbury Park, New Jersey. I was handed keys and was out the door, starting the engine of WABC Radio's bright white station wagon, with a yellow light on the roof, before I began to take stock. I was wearing a suit, shirt and tie—not exactly riot gear—and the station car wasn't what you'd call an undercover vehicle; it might make a terrific target for armed protesters. I had no two-way radio, just my Sony cassette machine and a bunch of dimes for the phone. My experience as a professional New York journalist totaled less than two months.

In 1970 things were tough along the Jersey shore: the number of summer jobs had been reduced by about half, and most remaining jobs were going to white youths. Asbury Park had also sharply cut summer recreation programs, so in the city's west side, located, literally, on the other side of the tracks, Black youngsters were faced with unemployment and nothing to keep them busy, while local government seemed unwilling to even talk about it.

I decided to park the WABC car on the quieter east side and walk toward the troubled section. It wasn't hard to find; you just headed toward the smoke. For the next three days my reports were featured on numerous WABC newscasts, and I did a 20-minute wrap-up for the "Perspective, NY" program. Some months later I learned that the Society of Silurians, a prestigious organization of journalists covering the Greater New York area, had selected my coverage of the Asbury Park story as the year's best Spot News Radio Reporting. Along with the renowned CBS-TV commentator Eric Sevareid, who won in the television category, I received my award from Mayor John Lindsay. It was one of several occasions when I achieved something wonderful before learning just how difficult it really was. I felt like the cartoon character who dashes off a cliff and is doing well running on thin air until a voice says, "Don't you know you can't do that?"

◆ ◆ ◆

WHEN MY SUMMER-RELIEF GIG AT WABC ended I was given a permanent job at the ABC Radio Network—a big operation, grinding out four newscasts per hour plus sports and other programs. My new boss was the brilliant managing editor Nick George, a fast-talking, pipe-smoking, two finger-typing journalist who not only loved news but studied the art of how to best write it for an audience of listeners rather than readers. The award-winning broadcaster Mort Crim once said, "Nick taught me more about good radio writing than all my professors. To this day I cannot bring myself to call a ship a vessel."

Nick's nemesis—and therefore mine—was the division's vice president, Tom O'Brien. Tom was a living cartoon. Rotund and red-faced, he was known behind his back as *The Pumpkin*. He made little effort to learn the names of people who worked for him—especially Nick's favorites—so he had the habit of calling everyone "Guy." As he collected his thoughts he preceded the greeting by making the sound, "Eeeeeeeee." Sometimes he would further embellish it with a term of faux endearment such as "scallywag." Thus, Tom might bound across the newsroom, stopping at the desk of someone he couldn't quite place, and thrust out his meaty palm while chortling: "Eeeeeeeee, my scallywag guy!"

A dominant feature of the newsroom was a ridiculous 30-foot map painted on an entire wall, with light bulbs all across it, ostensibly showing the path news took from points around the world to our headquarters. The switch controlling the lights was in Tom's office. With so many bulbs generating enormous heat and blinding light, the display was shut off most of the day. When it did come on it meant visiting VIPs were in the elevator and would soon be given a tour by Tom before heading off to an alcohol-heavy lunch. Sometimes when he returned, especially during the fall, there would be an actual pumpkin in front of his office door. Tom would have fit in perfectly at the Dunder Mifflin Paper Company.

♦ ♦ ♦

MY WORK AT ABC NEWS was an exciting, nonstop adrenaline fix. It was also exhausting, not just because of the deadlines but because there were no meal breaks or formal rest periods of any sort. We were expected to eat at our desks. ABC's massive news facility didn't have a commissary or snack bar; worse, it didn't even have a coffee pot. We were encouraged to have everything delivered, at our own expense, from various delis, Chinese restaurants and, with the greatest frequency, John's Coffee Shop on Broadway. Phone orders were placed every 30 minutes or so. A delivery guy, whose thick accent was almost always Greek or Chinese, would trot into the center of the newsroom—there was no security of any kind back then—and shout. It didn't seem to matter what language he was shouting in, since it all meant the same thing: your food is here...I'm in a hurry...tip generously.

Besides grueling hours and strange dining arrangements, the most debilitating part of working at ABC News was that the job never really stopped. Those of us who were Nick's top editors lived in constant fear of missing something, anything, of importance. We woke up early to scour newspapers at home, and arrived at the newsroom before our scheduled time to "read in" on news of the day. We monitored the competition on speakers at our desks and watched television screens that hung from the ceiling. My job grew even more demanding when Nick made me one of his weekend editors-in-charge. Working weekends had only two advantages: (a) No jacket and tie required, (b) Tom O'Brien worked Monday to Friday.

During my second year, Tom had a nervous fit when I turned up as a regular panelist on an all-night talk show at WMCA Radio, a gig that came about in a totally bizarre way.

Whenever I found it difficult to sleep, worried that news might break at any moment, I listened to the blandest talk radio I could find—not so much for content as for the melody of the voices. My favorite host was a character named Long John Nebel, who specialized in extended discussions about UFOs and conspiracy theories, none of which interested me. However, he was a great talker, a master salesman, and his commercials for "Ho Ho, the Chinese Restaurant" and "Mountain Valley Water," soothed me the way ocean sounds work for other people. One night Nebel was talking about marijuana. Although I didn't care for pot myself, and although I had never phoned a radio show (except to report that Colorado Women's College was ablaze) I picked up the phone. Soon I was on the air, anonymously, explaining to Nebel and his mostly older listeners how the drug business worked. Calls on the show typically lasted less than a minute; mine went on for about ten.

The following night, Nebel recounted the call. "I'd like to have heard more from that young man," he said. "If he's listening, I hope he will phone my producer in the morning." Really? I was stunned. Naturally, I phoned WMCA the next day and two nights later was an in-studio guest on "The Long John Nebel Show."

As odd as Nebel was on radio, he managed to be even more eccentric in person. His shtick for first-time guests, I discovered, began when his producer sat me in the studio a few minutes before airtime. I had no idea what Nebel looked like. What I saw was a painfully thin older gent with thick glasses, puttering around the studio, cleaning and dusting the microphones—a janitor I assumed. Then the red light came on and he dropped into the host's chair, catching me so off guard that Nebel had the upper hand he wanted for the entire show. We managed to talk about pot for the next hour, a bizarre exchange, since neither of us knew much about the topic.

The next day a producer phoned to ask if I'd care to join Nebel's cast of occasional contributors. I eagerly agreed, even though it meant staying up all night and not getting paid for it. Nebel's regulars were his friends and people who were willing to do the show for free in return for a chance to promote their business or book. I had nothing to plug. Meanwhile, word spread at ABC News that I was on Nebel's show, which worried Tom O'Brien so much that he ordered technicians in ABC's Master Control to record Nebel's broadcasts so he could replay them the next day. I suppose he feared I would say something critical of him or ABC News. Knowing that The Pumpkin sat through hours of nonsense about flying saucers and Ho Ho's menu, while I said not a word about ABC News, motivated me to keep doing Nebel's show.

Long John was not in good health and had a habit of leaving the studio in mid-discussion, without letting listeners know he was gone. It was incumbent upon the regulars to keep talking until he returned. One time, shortly after midnight on July 4, Nebel and I were alone on the air. He picked up the early edition of *The New York Times* and said, "Peter, you're a journalist. Why is the paper so thin on holidays?" Then he stood up and disappeared for what was roughly ten minutes. All I could think to say was that few advertisers cared to run ads on holidays, so the paper had fewer pages. I said it, in various ways, at least a dozen times—periodically adding, "as you know, John," making it seem as if he were with me in the studio.

Things got even stranger when Nebel married the former model Candy Jones and made her his co-host. I should note here that Nebel never seemed to connect my name with my father or "Candid Camera." This was in the early '70s when Dad's show had been off the air for a while. The thing is, three decades earlier, Dad had *dated* Candy Jones when she was with the Conover modeling agency. Nebel apparently didn't know that, and neither Candy nor I ever mentioned it. She was friendly but chilly, so after a few more appearances I stopped doing Nebel's show.

That freed up my time at night, and Tom O'Brien's during the day.

10 / (REALLY) ODD JOBS

IN MY FOURTH YEAR at ABC News I managed to get several feature articles published in *The New York Times* Sunday Arts and Leisure section, which prompted me to re-evaluate my career goals. Nick George had departed ABC a year earlier, leaving me suffering under Tom O'Brien and finding that telling Pumpkin jokes was getting old. Besides, the life of a freelance newspaper writer seemed attractive—working from home and setting my own schedule. So I quit my ABC job.

Overlooked in my haste was the fact that I was now without health insurance, union benefits or a weekly paycheck. Instead of elaborate orders for food to be delivered, I just walked a few feet to the refrigerator—with regrettable regularity. I visited the lobby at 11:15 each morning to check the mail, which was frequently the most exciting activity in my day. My girlfriend, Janice Clarke, had plenty of free time to look over my shoulder because she, too, quit her job at ABC News, much as Renee Zellweger left the sports agency as a show of support for Tom Cruise in the 1996 rom-com "Jerry Maguire."

At least, for the first time in my career, I wasn't working in a windowless newsroom. Now, I could gaze across a span of about eight feet as I typed for a delightful view of a concrete wall.

Not long after my breakthrough at *The Times* I managed to sell a piece to the *New York Daily News* Sunday Magazine in the category of journalism known as *human interest*. In this type of writing you take topics with no news value and craft them into stories with zero appeal. (For reasons readers have never figured out, editors are willing to pay for such stuff.) I was now writing what the "Seinfeld" crew would probably call "stories about nothing." My first concerned Samaritans who pick up litter. Yep, citizens who do good by cleaning up trash in parks and playgrounds. After that I wrote about how to get better seats at baseball games (example: bribe an usher to let you move closer to the field). I might have felt guilty passing such nothingness to readers were it not for the fact that *The News* paid me more than *The Times* did. I also signed on with *TV Guide* as a regular contributor. The weekly listings magazine, with a surprisingly vibrant editorial wrap-around, was at the peak of its popularity in the mid-70s, having attained a paid circulation of 19 million.

The relative ease with which I scored in early freelance efforts made me think about how my father struggled after college, trying to sell his own short stories to magazine editors. In desperation, he resubmitted several of his pieces to the same publications that had previously rejected them, but this time using an Asian-sounding pseudonym: Len Fu. All of a sudden he was making $25 per story. I briefly considered writing under the name Ter Fu, but fortunately I didn't need to do that.

My problem wasn't getting published so much as it was paying rent. *The Times* only paid a few hundred dollars for a full-length feature; *TV Guide* and the *Daily News* paid a bit more, but even with two or three published pieces per month the math didn't work. Most freelance writers are either, (a) in it for the ego boost, (b) married to someone earning a real salary, (c) angling for a full-time job—say, at ABC News, or (d) doing other things concurrently like lecturing or writing a book.

As mentioned in Chapter One (which was not a foreword), this led me to write the non-acclaimed book "Gotcha," which failed to generate much income.

Full disclosure: My family was fortunate to have plenty of money. But I was in the *prove-I-can-make-it-on-my-own* stage of life, sometimes referred to as the "starvation phase." I figured if I was writing for newspapers maybe I could also *sell* papers. A bit of background on that:

At age 11 I ran across an ad in the back of a comic book seeking boys to peddle a national tabloid with the distinctly non-newsy name *Grit* and the impressive slogan, "America's Greatest Family Newspaper." *Grit's* unique contribution to journalism began in 1884 when the German entrepreneur Dietrick Lamade bought the name and made *Grit* an independent weekly serving rural America. Lamade told his staff that *Grit* should, "*Avoid printing those things which distort the minds of readers or make them feel at odds with the world. Avoid showing the wrong side of things, or making people feel discontented. Do nothing that will encourage fear, worry, or temptation."*

It amazes me that in the 1880s they already knew so much about fake news. By 1932 *Grit's* circulation stood at 400,000; in the mid-fifties it reached 700,000, thanks to 30,000 young carriers. Circulation topped out in 1969 at 1.5 million.

One day the mailman brought a package with a canvas *Grit* delivery bag and my first shipment of 20 copies, to be sold door-to-door for ten cents each. This was no easy task. *Grit* was aimed at communities so rural that residents had little or no access to daily papers—not the case on Red Hill. Plus, in the New York City suburbs there wasn't a lot of interest in articles about how to oil a tractor or can peaches or whatever else came from an editorial staff that used the catchy slogan, "As American as mom, apple pie, and *Grit*."

I peddled *Grit* for about a month and I'd say my total sales were—and this is just an estimate—none. Moving on...

During summer vacation following 8th grade a man named Sal Verochi came around looking for kids to deliver a new morning paper called *Daily Trader*. I eagerly signed up and was given my canvas bag, route book and a sheaf of printed instructions dealing with such things as "always be polite to customers" and "get plenty of sleep." For the first two weeks *Daily Trader* was delivered at no charge to every house on the route, for which carriers got a penny a copy. Following this free trial, the paper had a cover price of five cents, and we were allowed to keep a penny and a half per copy.

Page one of *Daily Trader's* inaugural issue, Monday, Sept. 12, 1960, carried a headline that turned out to be an omen for both the publisher and me: HURRICANE HURLS WINDS NORTHWARD. It was Hurricane Donna, one of the most powerful Atlantic storms on record, causing over $400 million in damage. And there I was, standing in the storm at 5 a.m. on Mount Airy Road, wearing the yellow rain slicker Mom had purchased a day earlier. When there was still no sign of the delivery truck by 6:45, I sadly dried off, grabbed breakfast and took the bus to school.

By the time I returned home the sun was out, and there were three bundles of newspapers in our garage. I rushed out on my bike, dodging tree branches that littered the road, and knocked on every door to personally apologize and hand my customers their first copy of "Westchester's new morning paper!"

After two weeks of free sampling I revisited each home to find out how many families were willing to pay 30 cents a week as regular customers. Answer: 15. This turned out to be better than what most carriers achieved. I was one of *Daily Trader's* top delivery boys, now earning 22-and-half-cents a day for about 90 minutes work. (I have no idea what minimum wage was back then, but this wasn't it.)

While doing my route I was too busy to read the paper, so it wasn't until returning home on Saturday, Oct. 29, that I saw the headline that delivered a more painful blow than Hurricane Donna: DAILY TRADER TO CEASE PUBLICATION. Two days later Sal Verochi came to my house and retrieved my canvas bag and route book, plus the $3.15 I owed for the final week's papers.

So, now we jump ahead four years to summer vacation before I started college. I often went out in the evening to buy an early copy of the next day's *Daily News*—referred to by news buffs as the *bulldog edition*. Distribution of this edition was limited, and I began thinking it might be lucrative to sell bulldogs in bars throughout New York's northern suburbs. I drove to Manhattan and hung out in front of Grand Central Station, a few blocks from the News building, trying to figure out how I might purchase copies of the paper in bulk. Shortly before 7 p.m. a *News* truck arrived outside the 42nd Street entrance and began selling papers by the bundle. I learned this was how struggling storekeepers from all over Manhattan and the Bronx, who couldn't establish credit with the paper's circulation department, bought copies wholesale. I paid cash for 100 papers and headed north as fast as I could.

Adrenaline was surging as I pulled up to a tavern in Yonkers that seemed like as good a place as any to start. I went inside and announced: "Morning news! Tomorrow's *Daily News* tonight!" Two guys approached me a bit faster than I might have expected.

"Where's Shorty?" asked one man.

Unable to process this quickly enough to formulate an answer, I turned and bolted out the door. Puzzled more than shaken, I drove north to the more upscale town of Scarsdale and went into a restaurant-bar that seemed less threatening. And that's where I learned about Shorty . . .

It seems that Shorty, as he was known to his regular customers, was a middle-aged dwarf with a nasty limp, who sold bulldogs in bars across lower Westchester. But that was the least of it. Shorty was a numbers runner. Selling papers was a front for the Mob's Numbers Game—a kind of illegal lottery in which customers bet on a number and won a handsome payoff if the number came up. The number was determined by the last four digits of the take or "handle" at local racetracks. If, for instance, the handle at Belmont Park was $3,014,188, then the winning number that day would be 4188.

I drove home and placed 100 copies of the next morning's *Daily News* in the garage on Dad's stack of papers for the fireplace. What bad luck. Millions of people hadn't even discovered what would be in tomorrow's paper, and my copies were already piled up for burning. I suppose the good luck was that I never did run into Shorty or his well-connected friends.

SO, WE JUMP AHEAD TEN YEARS. I'm a 27-year-old ex-ABC staffer, struggling as a freelance writer and looking for extra money. Without giving it proper thought (my trademark), I find myself back in front of Grand Central Station, looking for the *Daily News* truck. It soon arrives and a cigar-smoking, barrel-chested guy stands on the back of the vehicle, about four feet off the ground, selling bundles of the next day's paper at wholesale to a line of men holding fist-fulls of crumpled cash.

I decided to take another crack at hawking bulldogs across my old stomping grounds in Westchester County. This time, however, I would do it only on Saturday nights; I'd avoid the type of establishments where mobsters like Shorty might be lurking, and now my girlfriend, Janice Clarke, would be riding shotgun (a figure of speech meaning she sat next to me, although having an actual gun might have made sense in this line of work). I didn't own a car, so I borrowed my sister Patty's blue VW Fastback—a bit larger than a

Beetle, but a tight squeeze for two adults and several hundred newspapers.

Among the more foolish things I tried was affixing a hand-lettered sign to the back of the car, declaring: STOP ME FOR THE SUNDAY NEWS! Of course, no one ever stopped me. What would anyone reading such a message on the rear of a VW take it to mean? Would they honk as one might for an ice cream truck?

The *Sunday News* had a cover price of 25 cents, and I paid 17 cents wholesale. Most people gave me a buck, so I was making 83 cents a copy, and after paying for gas had about $200 for a night's work—the type of cash income it made no sense to bother the IRS about.

The juxtaposition of things in my career was becoming surreal. Some Saturdays I was selling copies of papers in which an article with my byline was printed. (I bet Woodward and Bernstein never managed to do that.)

As my business grew, I began buying extra bulldogs at Gaynor News Co. in Mount Vernon, so I could fill Patty's car on 42nd Street and then reload in Westchester. Gaynor was one of a dozen newspaper wholesalers sharing the New York metro market, much as Vito Corleone and his colleagues divided territory in "The Godfather." It operated out of a rundown garage on Fourth Street, with a fleet of unmarked green trucks and dozens of highly-paid union drivers. The union was closed and all-white; jobs went to sons of existing members, despite the 1947 Taft-Hartley Act that prohibited such practices. In 1974 a Federal Court ordered the union to desegregate, but little changed.

When I approached Gaynor about bulldogs I was surprised there was a classification for what I hoped to do. It was "hustler." Of course, there hadn't been any news hustlers—guys who sold on street corners—in Westchester for many years, but Gaynor was happy to add my $500 security deposit to coffers that held large sums from every variety store, deli, gas station or other establishment in Westchester that sold newspapers. In some cases those deposits had been on the books for half a century.

The major papers had representatives known as *road men*, who divided their time between checking stores in the field and doing reports at Gaynor's office. They worked in the Road Room, a space on the second floor with a sloping wood floor, long wood counters with peeling paint that served as desks, black rotary phones and bare bulbs hanging from the ceiling. It was exactly what Hollywood would create in the unlikely event a film were ever to be made about newspaper wholesalers. The men themselves were straight from Central Casting—gravel-voiced Johnny DeAngelis of the *Daily News* and ruddy-faced Tom O'Connell of *The Times*.

Each Monday when I'd come to settle my account, Tom would buy me a cheese sandwich at the tiny coffee shop down the block. "*The Times* is starting distribution in vending machines," he said one day. "I thought maybe you would like to handle it." At the time none of the New York City papers had vending machines—those metal dispensers that in coming years would become ubiquitous (some would say eyesores) on the nation's sidewalks. Tom offered a $35 weekly subsidy, plus the regular per-copy profit on each copy sold. Without giving it proper thought (again, my trademark move), I said "sure."

Within days the blue and white *Times* machines appeared along Central Avenue, chained to light poles. These machines were known as "honor boxes" but really should have been called "theft boxes," because once you inserted coins and pulled open the door you had access to all the papers. A bigger problem: Neither Tom nor anyone at Gaynor News bothered to tell me that the drivers wouldn't allow a non-union scab like me to deliver papers. My new enterprise was delayed while a deal was made by which union drivers would deliver copies of *The Times* to each machine, leaving them tied and on the sidewalk, and then I would come along and place them in the machine. Of course, what the union really wanted—and got after a few days—was to have drivers be paid in full to *not* deliver to each machine. Once that was arranged, the union was more than willing to drop all my papers at a single location of my choosing: the all-night Raceway Diner on Yonkers Ave. With this settled, the *Daily News* and *Wall Street Journal* also acquired machines and paid me to service them.

Waking at 3 a.m. each day, I'd return, exhausted, to my Manhattan apartment by mid-afternoon. This went on six days a week in addition to the lucrative Sunday business, handled as it had been before by Janice and me (Sunday papers were too valuable to risk placing in honor boxes).

I was working 70 hours a week, with no days off, so doing freelance writing was out of the question.

At least I didn't have to worry about being stuck with unsold papers, of which there were many. Tom told me not to bother making returns the way stores did. All I had to do was come to the Road Room and fill out a sheet indicating how many I had sold; I could dispose of the unsold papers however I wanted.

I was getting a fuller picture of how the newspaper business worked. Everyone was, in effect, robbing everyone else. The drivers were doing whatever they could to cheat the wholesaler. The wholesaler was cheating the publishers and the publishers were, in turn, cheating advertisers with rates based on incorrect circulation figures. For my part, I didn't want to cheat; what I became good at was *estimating* how many papers I had sold. My fake numbers varied from week to week, but I always came out way ahead.

As for the actual unsold papers, I made a deal with the Pottery Barn in Elmsford to deliver them to its warehouse for wrapping glassware. I charged by the ton. With no idea what a ton of newspapers looked like, I estimated. I billed Pottery Barn for two tons one week and maybe 3.3 tons the next. At Christmas, when the store was desperate for newsprint, I ordered hundreds of extra papers from Gaynor and delivered the unopened bundles directly to Elmsford.

According to my best estimate, I made a lot of money.

SO, NOW WE MOVE TO THE "CAN THINGS GET ANY CRAZIER?" section of my self-employment history. . .

While delivering papers I was eating a lot of meals in diners. Like many customers waiting for their food, I often stared at the paper placemat, which might have had a lame puzzle or trivia question printed on it.

Inspired, I set up a company to produce placemats that were written, printed and distributed *daily* across Westchester. I called it *Newsmat*. The design mimicked an actual newspaper in miniature, with headlines and news reports, plus sports scores and the weather. Ads placed around the page would supposedly help support this endeavor. To free up time I hired two guys to work my vending route.

Of all the schemes and dreams I had pursued in my first 29 years, Newsmat was the most ambitious—and riskiest. Looking back, it's troubling but not surprising to recall how many news organizations praised Newsmat as a marvel of entrepreneurial effort—among them *The Wall Street Journal* and the Westchester-Rockland newspapers—without ever bothering to find out if I was making any money.

If a smart investor, say, one of the panelists on ABC's "Shark Tank," were running *Newsmat*, I'm sure his priorities would have been: (1) market aggressively, (2) sell as many ads as possible, and (3) find the cheapest way to get news reports. My priorities were: (1) hire a reporting staff and do exciting journalism, (2) spend lavishly to cover late-breaking news, (3) rent a nice office in White Plains, and (4) sell ads as time permits.

A few days after launch, I got a call from a reporter for the Sunday business section of the Westchester-Rockland newspaper chain, seeking to do a feature story. Under the headline, "A Bite to Eat and a Bit to Read," Michael Mudd's story noted, "It's hardly a publishing empire, but the fact that it costs next to nothing and is so clever makes it one to watch." He also reported on our color scheme:

> *Funt wanted to make sure that fresh mats were used each day and not hold overs from the day before so he arranged to have Newsmat printed on different color stock for each day of the week. "Monday is blue, Tuesday is yellow, and so on," Funt explains. "It was going fine until we got to Thursday. Thursday was goldenrod, and I got endless phone calls telling me goldenrod runs when it's wet. I've got to replace goldenrod."*

My 40 restaurants were only paying a dollar a day for *Newsmat*, so the bulk of revenue had to come from advertising. But I was focused on the journalism which, for a placemat editor, is an exotic preoccupation. I hoped for news to break between midnight and 8 a.m.—too late for the morning papers yet in time for *Newsmat's* deadline.

Our biggest story happened on the night of August 10, 1977, when Yonkers police arrested the "Son of Sam." Police announced the news after midnight and the newspapers missed out. It was one of the rare times I took a byline:

.44 KILLER ARRESTED IN YONKERS
"Well, you've got me!"...Parking Ticket Broke Case
By Peter Funt

One of the largest manhunts in criminal history ended last night outside an apartment building in Yonkers when police arrested a 24-year-old postal worker who they say is Son of Sam—the .44-caliber killer.

The suspect, David Berkowitz, was arrested without incident at about 10:15 p.m. at 35 Pine Street, where he calmly told officers: "Well, you've got me."

My 650-word story occupied much of the page. It's too bad there are

Westchester-Rockland papers printed this photo of me in the pressroom, with copies of my money-losing placemats ready for news-hungry readers.

no awards for placemat journalism because I feel certain *Newsmat* would have won in the category of *Most Gruesome News During Lunch.*

◆ ◆ ◆

DID I MENTION THAT I WAS LOSING MONEY?

Trying to save my placemat business, I made overtures to two big companies that were seeking to grow early morning traffic. Dunkin' Donuts considered it, but passed. However, McDonald's was willing to give *Newsmat* a try in Manhattan.

By 1978 McDonald's had served over 20 billion hamburgers and was adding a full line of breakfast foods including the Egg McMuffin (the breakfast food I imagine people in other countries cite most often when asked about "stupid American dietary choices"). McDonald's agreed to buy a customized version of *Newsmat*, to be titled *McDonald's NY Report*, as a test in a dozen stores. After five weeks the trial was declared an overwhelming success. Alas, McDonald's bean counters decided to save money by buying "entertain-ment-calendar placemats" (cheaper because their content only changed once a month), from a supplier in New Jersey.

My McDonald's deal was dead and so was *Newsmat.*

Today, of course, when you visit a McDonald's you see people staring at mobile devices, reading digital news. Few of them, trust me, are scrolling through monthly "entertainment calendars."

On the plus side: With *Newsmat* I experienced being the best in the world at doing something—in this case writing news on placemats—even if I happened to be the *only* person in the world caring to try it. I also learned that I had misjudged the guy whose company printed *Newsmat.* Turns out Mike Antonelli did have a sense of humor.

Each morning after unlocking the place at 4 a.m. I had to walk past Mike's desk to get to the coffee maker. One day I saw a folded sheet of paper on which was written CONFIDENTIAL. I took a few more steps. But, heck, it was 4 a.m., I was the only person in the place, and the paper on Mike's desk wasn't sealed, only folded. I lifted it just enough to read the message inside, about which I laugh to this day.

It said: *Good morning, Peter!*

With my placemat operation gone I figured I should get out of the newspaper delivery business as well. A classified ad brought a few interested buyers, one of whom I came to refer to as "Mister What's to Prevent?" Barry Lass was a worrier. He rode with me on the route, firing a barrage of questions that all began the same way: "What's to prevent people from taking more than one copy?" "What's to prevent papers from getting wet in the rain?" "What's to prevent publishers from cutting the subsidy?"

This went on for more than a week until one morning at the Mister Donut shop I said, "Barry, what's to prevent me from selling to someone else?" He handed me his check for $10,000 and that was the last I heard of him.

Unfortunately, it wasn't the last I heard of the mobsters at Gaynor News. They presented me with a final bill of $9,200.

◆ ◆ ◆

SO, WE JUMP AHEAD ONE MONTH ...

With new-found free time, Janice and I spent a day visiting Bear Mountain State Park across the Hudson River, north of Peekskill. It has an abundance of pine trees and we filled a bag with pine cones and brought them home. I don't know what possessed me, but a few days later I showed them to a florist on Madison Avenue. "How much?" he asked. With no clue about what might qualify as a reasonable answer I *estimated,* "Ten bucks." As I took his money I noticed that the shop had dried-flower arrangements on display, made from the kind of stuff I had seen growing wild at Bear Mountain and, for that matter, along the Hutchinson River Parkway and other public places in Westchester. The next day I became a fulltime pine cone and dried-weeds wholesaler.

I'd start out early each morning (that's what we farmers do), scouring roadsides for anything that resembled what I had seen in the florist's store. I'd cut, pick, batch and bundle whatever looked good, being alert for poison ivy, the occasional snake, or overly-curious municipal workers. That last group proved to be indifferent to my efforts, since all I was doing was removing weeds that they would eventually have to clear themselves.

I *harvested* as much as would fit into my Toyota Celica and set out to sell to shops on the Upper East Side. I learned: (1) florists will, indeed, pay cash to an uncredentialed hustler if they like the looks of whatever he's selling, (2) when it comes to dried stuff, as opposed to fresh flowers, florists are seriously clueless, and (3) no one knows what weeds should cost.

Particularly attractive were cattails, the tall, slender marsh plants topped with a distinctive brown cylinder that is the furry flower of the plant. Florists paid me a dollar or more for a single clean, sturdy cattail. That sparked an idea: I placed a classified ad inviting people to bring their cattails to a parking lot where I'd be paying 25 cents apiece. It would have made a funny sequence on "Candid Camera": folks of varied ages arrived with all sorts of plants, only about half of which were cattails. Many of the specimens were moldy or disfigured. I assume serious trespassing had been going on during the hunting and gathering process—but I didn't care to ask. I purchased several hundred cattails and headed to Manhattan.

Nature's plan for this plant is that the brown cylindrical part will eventually burst open to release cottony seeds. This happens naturally in fall, but can be accelerated by warmth, say, in the back of a Toyota. By the time I reached the Upper Eastside half of my cattails had exploded. (The pro trick, I learned later, is to pick them at the peak of firmness and then seal them with hairspray.)

By Thanksgiving there was little left to harvest, but still many pine cones to gather. (Did you know that the pine cone is the state flower of Maine, even though it's not actually a flower?)

Janice and I took to making Christmas wreaths from pine cones, attaching them with thin wires to round metal frames. We managed to sell our wreaths to boutiques and other retail shops as seasonal window decorations, getting $100 a pop. The best looking cones were the large "sugar" variety that got their glistening appearance from sap. After hours of wreath-making our hands glistened as much as the cones, and our fingers felt permanently welded together.

I only spent one season as a dried-weed wholesaler, but I learned an important lesson for anyone who cares to give it a try: Florists will buy more and pay higher prices for things that have names. So, I made sure to name everything I sold. My wispy pale yellow weeds became *Fantasia*. The dark brown stalks with tiny dried flowers were *Prairie Thistle*.

One other thing: Once you've had this experience you'll never again be able to drive past cattails swaying in the breeze without imagining that affixed to each stem is a dollar bill.

11 / CABLE GUY

MY SISTER PATTY WAS DATING A NICE GUY named Warren Schomaker, originally from Australia and 27 years her senior. Adding to his appeal, he was a multi-millionaire. Warren conducted his business from a beautifully furnished co-op on Park Avenue. The first time I visited he pointed to several over-sized ceramic bowls of potpourri, placed decoratively on tables in the front hall, living room and bedroom. "Look at this," he said proudly, pushing aside a thin layer of potpourri to reveal his stash of silver dollars—thousands of them, squirreled away throughout the apartment. "I trust banks," he explained, "but only to a point."

Warren had made millions buying and selling small telephone companies in rural America and now he and his partners were rushing into cable television. In some remote areas they simply laid cable on the ground along the road, without the annoying expense of utility poles. Warren knew of my interest in journalism and had read my pieces in *The Times*. He also loved my sister, so perhaps it was Patty more than my writing that prompted him to offer me the well-paying job of Marketing Director at Omni Cable TV Corp.

This proved to be very much like selling Fantasia to florists: I knew nothing about cable and, back then, neither did our customers. Adding to the confusion, cable viewers had no idea what was on or when. I sketched out plans for a monthly magazine that would provide listings along with meaningful journalism about cable's new world. I called it *ON CABLE Magazine.*

Warren's fondness for my sister notwithstanding, it took a lot of chutzpah to propose that he give me several million dollars to launch a national magazine. The sum total of my publishing experience was printing news on placemats. Incredibly, perhaps after too many cocktails at lunch, Omni's board of directors voted to back my magazine, with me as editor and publisher.

◆ ◆ ◆

THIS MIGHT BE A GOOD TIME to review the writings of Canadian scholar Dr. Lawrence J. Peter in his 1968 book "The Peter Principle." The major conclusion is that employees rise within a company through promotion until they reach a level of incompetence. Dr. Peter also explained that the employee's inability to meet the requirements of a new position might be due to the fact that the job requires different skills than the employee actually possesses. (My take on this is: I wish the guy had not been named Peter.)

◆ ◆ ◆

ALTHOUGH WARREN CONTINUED to work from his apartment, I moved into space alongside Omni's financial team in a renovated warehouse near the railroad tracks in Norwalk, Connecticut. I placed classified ads in the *Norwalk Hour* for two "editorial assistants" and about a dozen eager applicants showed up. I picked two: Cathy Mantegna and Barbara Jean Iacuzio, neither of whom had any experience in publishing, cable television, or dealing with a guy like me. We occupied two small rooms next to Omni's accountants, who took every opportunity to point out that risking so much money on a half-baked fantasy was beyond insane.

A typical magazine start-up might take several years, during which time there would be market research, prototypes, public relations and advertising presentations. We did none of that, and we had just three months to prepare our first issue. The debut cover wasn't about new shows that were on that month (which would have made sense). Instead, it featured an eye-catching color illustration by air-brush wizard Todd Schorr, who had done posters for George Lucas and Francis Ford Coppola. I paid Todd $1,200 of Omni's money to depict aliens on a distant planet watching cable TV. The story, with the headline "Where Is Satcom III?" was about the failed launch of a communications satellite. It was solid reporting but not exactly what marketing people might have advised to lure new cable subscribers or please existing ones. Also on the first cover: "How HBO Compiles Secret Ratings," a compelling story, but perhaps better suited for a trade publication. As with *Newsmat*, I was so eager to convince skeptics that the public would support solid journalism over pablum that I pushed too hard.

ON CABLE'S circulation grew exponentially, some months adding 50,000 copies or more. Printing had to be moved from a small plant on Long

Island to one of the largest, state-of-the-art facilities in the country, operated by RR Donnelley & Sons in Glasgow, Kentucky. Our business became so complicated that I needed to hire high-priced consultants, the most renowned being James B. Kobak.

Jim's career in publishing went back to 1946. He became the industry's leading guru after developing "The Kobak Model," a secret formula used to predict ad sales, circulation and revenue for magazine start-ups. Publishers like me would give Jim our raw data, plus a check to cover his exorbitant fee, and he would return a week or so later with impressive charts showing...

Well, that was the interesting thing about The Kobak Model: it seemed to show whatever you wanted it to show. If you needed "X" to persuade an investor, or "Y" to raise capital, the Model would give it to you—and with James B. Kobak's signature, it was accepted as gospel.

Jim was an eccentric man, whose oddest habit was wearing short pants no matter what the occasion or the weather. It could have been 15 degrees in January and Jim would walk into our office wearing a heavy knit sweater with shorts—not even down to the knee; they were closer to the length of bathing trunks. I once brought Jim to a boardroom in Manhattan to meet with my investors. Everyone was in suits and ties, except Jim, who looked as if he were about to go hiking in the Alps. Years after I worked with Jim he wrote a book with the succinct title, "How to Start a Magazine." I didn't learn much from reading it, but one chapter had a name that rang true: "Starting a Magazine Is Like Nothing You Have Ever Done Before, Even If You Have Done It Before."

◆ ◆ ◆

NOW, A WORD ABOUT CATS...

During my years working really odd jobs, stray cats played a key role.

One frigid December morning during my newspaper delivery days I was filling a vending machine at the Greystone railroad station in Yonkers when a black cat crossed my path. She was a kitten, actually, and visibly underfed. I asked if anyone knew about her and learned she was a feral rail yard resident. So, I put her in my car.

It turned out that Sweetie liked route work, but what she really loved were treats from the fridge at my Manhattan apartment, as well as the softness of my bed. There is no better friend than a rescued animal.

The following summer, I was sitting at the counter in the Mister Donut shop on Central Avenue late on a Saturday night, drinking free coffee and schmoozing with the counter girl, when a car screeched into the parking lot. There was a thud, followed by another screech as the vehicle sped away. We ran outside to find a tiny gray kitten, who had been thrown against a fence.

After I paid $300 in vet bills, I discovered that Donut loved route work, my New York apartment, and Sweetie. The two rescued felines became soulmates.

A few years later, driving up Madison Avenue one morning on my way to *ON CABLE*, I hit the brakes in the intersection at 125th Street. A kitten had run into the street and seemed to disappear under my car. A crowd formed and split into two noisy factions: one insisted I drive on and stop blocking the intersection, the other warned me not to move until the cat could be rescued. After a few tense minutes I crawled under the car, grabbed the kitten, and plopped him on the passenger's seat. Upon reaching Norwalk he was nowhere to be seen, but meowing noises were coming from inside the dashboard. Three editors grabbed tools and over the course of the next hour helped me disassemble the entire dashboard until we finally discovered the confused gray kitten behind the clock.

After $800 in vet bills had been paid, Dasher made himself at home at *ON CABLE* as our company mascot. According to the Rule of Three, I had reached my feline quota.

FROM THE DEPARTMENT of Anything That Can Go Wrong Will, Warren Schomaker lost control of Omni Cable, and the company's new bosses had no interest in being publishers, and even less in losing money. *ON CABLE* had grown to 655,000 monthly circulation, but doing so had cost Omni $4.3 million. We had a problem that meteoric start-ups often face: funding growth while waiting for revenue to catch up. In October, 1982, as we prepared the November issue, Omni's new president, John McCormick, closed us down.

The staff was in shock but everyone agreed to work without pay while I tried to figure something out. With less than 24 hours before our production deadline—and with no money to pay for printing—I arranged a 9 p.m. meeting at the Park Avenue offices of Warburg Pincus Capital Corp., one of the nation's most powerful venture capital firms.

I had never met anyone at Warburg and knew absolutely nothing about the world in which it operated. What I did know, from Warren and people like Jim Kobak, was that they had plenty of money and loved making stealthy financial maneuvers. I sat in a waiting room while an executive named Sid Lapidus read my proposal. When he emerged at 10:30 Sid asked, "Did you write this?" I nodded, and he drafted a letter to be delivered by bonded courier to the home of John McCormick. It said Warburg would pay $100,000 for a 30-day option to purchase 100 percent of *ON CABLE*, and that production was to continue on the November issue.

It was after midnight when I caught the last train to Norwalk. I'm sure if cell phones had existed I would have phoned someone to explain the inexplicable: My magazine had been saved with hours to spare, we'd continue our mission, and I'd have a new partner who understood the need to spend money to make money.

My train slid through the Park Avenue tunnel, right under the offices of Warburg Pincus where, it seemed to me, a miracle had occurred.

All of a sudden, *ON CABLE* was a hot property and several suitors requested meetings. One was at the office of the magazine world's favorite bad boy at the time: Jann Wenner, co-founder and publisher of *Rolling Stone*. Wenner's company was looking for ways to branch out. I was surprised when he handed me a detailed stack of financials for the parent company, Straight Arrow. It was as if he hoped I would invest in *Rolling Stone*, but really it was just a reflection of Jann Wenner's maverick, free-wheeling approach to business—in fact, to life in general. Another meeting was in the richly paneled and polished office of Katharine Graham at *The Washington Post*. The Post Company owned television stations and was getting into cable; it also published Newsweek magazine. My brief chat with Mrs. Graham and my session with her son Donald didn't amount to much, but the Grahams couldn't possibly have known what it meant to me to walk their hallowed halls.

And then there was a dinner I had with a top vice president from Time Inc. named Larry Crutcher, who was about to launch a magazine to compete with *ON CABLE*. My staff had grown impressively to 40 people—if you count me and Tony Dudley the mailroom guy. *TV-Cable Week*, as Time called its imitation, had 42 managers on its staff—12 with Harvard credentials, 3 with Yale degrees, and 2 holding degrees from Columbia. Yet here I was sitting across from Larry Crutcher at pricey Cinquante Cinq restaurant in Greenwich, listening to him: (a) insist that *TV-Cable Week* would be a winner, (b) concede to having editorial and marketing problems, and (c) probe about whether *ON CABLE* was for sale. I didn't care for the meal (no pasta on the menu), or for Crutcher's offer to buy *ON CABLE*, which I flatly rejected. But I left satisfied that Time's venture was in trouble and we could survive.

TV-Cable Week had its debut a few months later. It would be unfair of me to comment on its quality, so I'll quote from a review in the *Village Voice:*

"Probably never in the history of the printed word has so much money produced so little content as the dreck contained in the first two issues of *TV-Cable Week*. ... Even casual exposure to the contents of *TV-Cable Week* would give anyone without a lobotomy a real appreciation for the copy on the back of cereal boxes."

TV-Cable Week folded after six months, with direct cash losses of $47 million plus a hit to Time's stock of nearly $750 million in market value. I ran an ad in *The New York Times* with the headline:

ON CABLE: WE'VE PASSED THE TEST OF TIME.

CABLE PROGRAMMING EXECUTIVES were frequently unhappy with our edgy, sometimes critical, reporting. HBO was especially vexed and sent one of its marketing managers to lobby for more positive coverage. I hated such meetings and usually had our editors handle them, but as I watched Amy Meltzer walk from her car she certainly looked more attractive than most of the network flacks I was used to fending off. I sent Dasher down the hall to sniff her out, because you can tell a lot about people by how they react to the presence of a cat in a business office. I also asked my assistant Donna for a report and got a thumbs up. So, we went to lunch with two of my editors, who watched in fascination as Amy and I sparred over my adamant refusal to compromise editorial integrity—and to debate just about every topic that came up, from the menu to the weather. The two editors said it was like watching Sam and Diane's flirtatious bickering on an episode of "Cheers."

A few days later I took Amy to hear Woody Allen play clarinet at Michael's Pub in New York. We argued for an hour about whether Sharon Stone appeared in "Manhattan" or "Stardust Memories."

Seven months later we were engaged.

Amy is a terrific combination of brains and beauty (and I believe I would say that even if she weren't proofreading this book prior to publication). She's been a great mother to Stephanie and Danny. She (usually) tolerates my hectic schedule as well as my desire to watch sports while eating dinner. If I had to cite just one tiny flaw in what is now a 35-year relationship, it's that Amy and I have practically nothing in common. Maybe that promotes longevity. It certainly keeps things interesting. (Does that sound accurate, Amy?)

♦ ♦ ♦

AMONG MY SPECIAL PLEASURES at *ON CABLE* was writing an April Fool's column, one of which, in 1982, was covered this way by *The Washington Post*:

> "Richard Hack, a daily gossip spieler for Metromedia's syndicated 'Breakaway' program, went on the air yesterday with some hot flashes about what he described as Michael Jackson's upcoming 'Tingle' video, a three-minute bit that he said would feature Jackson emerging from a boutique in a purple evening gown and catching fire, all with huge spin-offs in film and video and, of course, all for huge amounts of money.

> "Turns out that 'Tingle' is the brainchild of Peter Funt, editor and publisher of *ON CABLE Magazine.* And for the last four years, Funt has written an April Fool's piece. This year, it was about Jackson and his $50 million 'Tingle.' And Hack was the Fool. Hack, slightly put out, says he never saw the article."

By the end of 1985 *ON CABLE'S* circulation topped 1.5 million and monthly ad revenue climbed above $250,000. But it remained very expensive to fund our growth. Cox Communications decided to buy out Warburg and me and merge our magazine with its profitable broadcast division. To our utter shock and dismay, two days later we were shut down so Cox could take a big write-off. It was an odd end to a five-year run that had gone so well—for me and my hard working team. In my final column, I recalled a remark Dick Cavett once made when his TV series was canceled. "'South Pacific' closed," he said, "but no one ever called it a flop."

Cox had paid me $100,000 and I decided to risk it all on a new venture called "Cable Tonight." I would produce short TV features for interstitial use by cable systems—sort of a miniature video version of *ON CABLE*. In another of my "Jerry McGuire" moments, I asked who on the magazine's staff would come with me, and the only person willing to take the gamble was Allison Bansak from accounting. On our first day I asked Allison why she had placed such confidence in me. "I'm four months pregnant," she said, "and my husband and I really need the insurance coverage." I explained that she was my lone employee and that I had no insurance. Making matters worse, it was January and the landlord apparently had no plans to provide heat. However, I assured Allison that I'd cover all expenses for her and her baby, and I rushed out to buy space heaters.

We shot "Cable Tonight" at the Westinghouse studios in Stamford, with Lou Volpicelli of "Monday Night Football" as director.

This went on for a year, during which time Allison had her baby and feedback on my show was great. But without satellite distribution, which I couldn't afford, the concept wouldn't work; we were shipping three-quarter inch video tapes around the country—a tedious and dated process. Once out of money, I closed "Cable Tonight."

And so ended a ten-year odyssey in which I wrote for newspapers while also delivering them . . . published restaurant placemats and ate off them . . . picked weeds in order to sell them . . . watched my magazine blossom and then die . . .made a lot of money and lost it all.

With this came many life-lessons, which I'm determined to someday figure out.

12 / HOMEWORK

TOO TIRED TO DRIVE back to Manhattan one night during a hectic period at *ON CABLE*, I checked-in to a Howard Johnson's near my office. Seven months later, I checked out.

I can't imagine what the motel staff thought was going on in Room 127. I'm surprised they didn't have cops check for dead bodies.

In fact, during my seven-month odyssey a "sheriff" did show up 45 miles away, at my New York apartment. Unlike, say, Mayberry, where the sheriff was an upstanding guy who took his son fishing and rushed home for his aunt's apple pie, the New York City sheriff—at least back in the 1980s—was a flunky. (Wikipedia: "deputies perform a wide array of tasks such as evictions, warrants of arrest, orders to commit, and the seizure and sale of property pursuant to judicial mandates.")

The scheme went like this: A notice was placed on my door regarding "abandonment" of the premises. A neighbor phoned after seeing the note and I rushed home. Everything I owned was gone—right down to a signed Mickey Mantle photo and my childhood stamp collection. I called the sheriff's department and was told that my stuff was "in storage" in the Bronx. A deputy said that "drugs and related paraphernalia" had been seized (not true); however, if I paid $5,000 this unfortunate "misunderstanding" could be corrected. After coughing up the money I rented a U-Haul and drove to the Bronx. The "storage" facility was a rat-infested dump, and all that remained of my possessions were two broken chairs and a mattress.

I hired a lawyer not named David Dufus Esq. and attempted to sue the City of New York. This dragged on for several months, during which time I paid legal fees of about $10,000. A subsequent phone conversation went like this:

ME: So, where are we?

DUFUS: Well, as I'm sure you know it's very difficult to sue the City.

ME: Right.

DUFUS: If it were me, I'd walk away.

ME: If it were you, would you have paid a lawyer $10,000 to learn that?

DUFUS: I've tried to act in your best interests.

ME: So, are you returning my money?

DUFUS: No, that's something we don't do.

Fearing that I'd be billed for the call, I hung up. I also permanently "abandoned" my apartment. (I'd say I "moved out," but since I already had the mattress and chairs, there was nothing to move.)

BY THE TIME I MARRIED AMY I was living in a rented house in Rowayton, Connecticut, with my three cats. With her cat Rusty we now had enough claw power to destroy all shapes and styles of furniture.

I saw an ad for a house in the neighboring community of New Canaan that should have been headlined: *If it seems too good to be true, it probably is.* We bought the place within minutes after the real estate agent showed us the long winding driveway, the large lawn and the spectacular pond. Alas, I should have paid closer attention a few years earlier when Richard Benjamin made the movie "The Money Pit," with Tom Hanks starring as me, and Shelley Long playing Amy. Our house had no heat or air conditioning. The previous owners had somehow survived Connecticut winters by huddling near a wood-burning stove, but on the glorious 75-degree autumn day when I signed the contract, heat never crossed my mind. What I really loved was that big pond. However, when summer arrived the pond developed green scum so thick I think you could have walked across it—that is, if you dared challenge the mosquitoes and giant snapping turtles. I hired all sorts of experts to rescue my pond, and one guy suggested buying certain Japanese fish that for some twisted reason enjoy eating pond scum. The downside, he explained, was that they're expensive, illegal, and likely to escape unless barricades were built to keep them from swimming downstream to the neighbors' scum-covered ponds. Meanwhile, the heating guy talked me into acquiring heat pumps for the house. Heat pumps, I later learned, work fairly well in places like Georgia where the temperature rarely dips below 40 degrees. My heat pumps were installed and roaring away when I realized that on many fall and winter nights in Connecticut the temperature drops into the 20s or lower, and I wasn't pumping much heat, only an epic electric bill.

Our New Canaan house had many of the same problems Tom Hanks' place had, from lousy plumbing to "weak trees." We also had the very same contractors who cheerfully predicted all jobs would take "two weeks," while knowing it would be at least two months before work even started.

We had nine rooms and enough furniture for two. Faced with this problem, I decided I would invest all my time and money building a "playroom" in the basement for three-year-old Stephanie and three-month-old Danny. When designer-dressed New Canaan mothers from the "Playgroup" came over, they and their kids were whisked through the unfurnished spaces and into the playroom—a windowless cave, without heat or airflow of any kind, where the odor of fresh paint and new carpet never seemed to dissipate.

Our New Canaan adventures were brusquely interrupted when my father suffered a stroke and I flew out to California to help with his care. I thought I'd be gone for a few days, but after three weeks I sent for Amy and the kids. We never went back. I sold the Connecticut house by phone —!—and hired a company to pack our stuff and drive it to California. We bought a house about a mile from Dad's place in Pebble Beach—the scenic oceanside community in Central California.

Before making too many snide comments about Pebble Beach and the politically conservative zillionaires who have second or third McMansions there, let me say it is, indeed, beautiful, and I'm fortunate to live in such a place.

One of the first things I learned was that residents were required to have wooden mailboxes designed like bird houses. This supposedly gave streets a quaint, uniform look. It also provided local teens with something to do at night: driving around at high rates of speed and smashing mailboxes with baseball bats. Replacement boxes could only be found at one hardware store in town, and as I purchased my third mailbox in two months I couldn't help but wonder how many neighborhood teens the store owner had on his payroll.

As quirky as Pebble Beach is, the adjacent municipality of Carmel-by-the-Sea is even quirkier. It has no street addresses (houses are located by descriptions such as, "Stone house, third up the hill on the right"). This would have created a nightmare for the Postal Service were it not for the fact that Carmel doesn't allow home-delivered mail. (Residents pick up their mail at the post office.) Houses are even more difficult to locate at night because Carmel doesn't have any street lights. That's a safety problem, as is the fact that Carmel also doesn't have traffic signals. What it does have is a law prohibiting high heels. Anyone wishing to wear a heel higher than two inches, or narrower than one square inch, is required to obtain a permit (a law police no longer enforce).

Strange stuff, but what would you expect from a community that in 1986 elected Clint Eastwood mayor?

WHILE I DON'T BELIEVE IN GATED COMMUNITIES, I felt Pebble Beach's five gates would provide security for Amy and the kids. It's a nifty arrangement. Crooks are forbidden from entering Pebble Beach unless they pay the $10.50 "gate fee" (which comes with a handy map of the territory). To supplement this airtight security arrangement I paid an alarm company to wire my house. Clearly the money was well spent because, as of this writing, we've only been robbed twice.

The first burglary was a straightforward break-in, triggering the alarm—which both the thieves and my security company chose to ignore. The second incident occurred while we were 100 miles away in San Francisco for Stephanie's wedding. As I took Steph's hand to walk her down the aisle, my cell phone vibrated with news from the alarm company that our house was experiencing what the operator called "an active event."

ME: So am I.

SHE: What would you like us to do?

ME: I thought you people know what to do.

SHE: We need to ascertain if you're inside the dwelling.

ME: I'm not! Call the police!

SHE: Your tone is very disrespectful.

ME: Look, I'm at my daughter's wedding, and I can't ... hello?

Neighbors told us that even before the burglars arrived other thieves had stolen five cartons of wedding gifts that Crate & Barrel had left on our porch.

On the brighter side: I received an unsolicited email from Facebook inviting me to join the neighborhood's "Crime Watch Group."

I also screened an old Woody Allen monologue in which he suggested placing a sticker on the front door saying: WE GAVE.

◆ ◆ ◆

THE LOCAL SPCA is on my speed dial. This is because I have a lifelong pattern of finding animals in need, and an equally lengthy history of not knowing what to do with them. (You're probably asking, "What's the difference between SPCA and ASPCA?" Wikipedia: "ASPCA works under one banner and has the same aims and objectives. SPCA has different goals and targets in each country and are not connected to each other in any way.")

Let's start with deer, which are as numerous in Pebble Beach as golfers, although they don't wear plaid. I could have saved myself hours of worry and several calls to the SPCA had I read this blog by Native Animal Rescue:

> Healthy baby fawns are daily left alone by their mothers while the mothers forage for food. Unfortunately, many times a lone fawn is picked up by people who mistakenly think the fawn has been abandoned. ... Kidnapped fawns should be immediately returned to the exact location where they were found and left alone.

Who could have known that? When I encountered a fawn in front of our house I panicked because it was so close to the street. I searched in the garage for orange traffic cones. Finding none, I settled for a folding beach chair which I placed in the road to force cars to steer clear. The SPCA operator kept urging me to remain calm but, despite her advice, Amy and I encouraged the baby to move onto our driveway, making us accomplices in a kidnapping. In late afternoon the mother came by and nonchalantly picked up the baby, as if

late for soccer practice.

Then there were the two crows I discovered on the street. The older bird was dead; the younger, we'll call him Frankie, was standing guard and wouldn't budge. I moved the dead bird off the pavement hoping the little guy would follow. But Frankie, about three or four weeks old and unable to fly, held his ground. So I took him home and Googled "caring for young crows and ravens."

Seems these birds make good pets, provided they are introduced to people before being "imprinted" in the wild. I also learned that they're quite messy, often moody, and will eat just about anything. One site said for young-sters you must "place a glob of food on your finger and push it down the crow's throat." (I wish I had video of my failed attempts at doing this with Frankie.)

Amy suggested I phone the SPCA, sending me into immediate panic. What if Frankie wound up being euthanized in a dingy back room, where I envisioned all the "lesser" critters went eventually?

Martha, in the Wildlife Department, was surprisingly sympathetic (clearly unaware I was wanted for an earlier deer kidnapping). She said one of her colleagues was only a few miles from my house and could be over in a few minutes.

She'd come to me? In a few minutes? Good luck getting such service from a plumber.

Jen arrived in a very official-looking truck and put on surgical gloves. She gave Frankie an exam and pronounced him fit, but too underfed to be returned to the wild. Jen took Frankie to headquarters where, I was assured, he'd be eating a mixture of cat food and raw vegetables.

I began having second thoughts about a column I had written in *USA Today* suggesting that it was unwise to donate to causes other than human services while so many Americans were hungry. I mumbled something to Jen about making a donation, which she politely said wasn't necessary.

Every living thing deserves our sympathetic attention, especially those who, by chance, are placed in our paths—Donut and Dasher among them.

The columnist in me wants to say I was forced to eat crow, but the creature-lover in me would rather not.

♦ ♦ ♦

OUR BACKYARD IS USUALLY FILLED with sounds of birds, frogs, crickets and teens down the street testing their new cars. Occasionally there is also the haunting sound of raccoons laughing at me.

When we moved to Pebble Beach, I wondered why neighbors were so protective of their trash that they secured garbage cans with bungee cords and even padlocks. Seems raccoons love trash, so I drilled holes in our cans and installed industrial strength locks. That's when I discovered raccoons also love lawns.

If you haven't seen what a squad of raccoons can do to a lawn, imagine a bunch of huge sardine cans, each about three feet long, with the lids peeled back. Or, a dozen bald heads, each about three feet wide, with toupees pulled off and tossed to the side.

Eventually I had to hire a lawn guy.

"You've got raccoons," Ralph announced, with the same smugness I recall my dentist using when he told me I had impacted wisdom teeth. He sold me high-priced replacement sod without mentioning that new turf doesn't discourage raccoons, it actually attracts them.

This led me to the hardware store, where Ernie explained my options. You can shoot 'em (out of the question); poison 'em (equally unacceptable), or trap 'em. The trap I bought is rather plush—in fact I once sat next to a woman on a four-hour plane ride who had her dachshund in a far less comfortable looking container. The trick, of course, is to persuade a raccoon to go inside. "They'll eat anything," Ernie assured me. Anything, it turns out, except garbage. I baited my trap with the very same type of garbage that raccoons had knocked over trash cans to get, and they wouldn't touch it. So I began experimenting with raccoon cuisine, resulting in a tempting assortment of peanut butter sandwiches and honey-covered apples. A nightly refrain in our kitchen was, "Don't touch that! It's for the raccoons."

One morning I discovered we had a chubby raccoon in our trap. Seems that once the sun comes up, and after digesting several peanut butter sandwiches, raccoons are fairly subdued. I drove the guy, whom we'll call Frankie, in his comfy airline-quality carrier to a wooded area about three miles away. The next night I caught Frankie's friend. Then his friend's friend. And this continued until a total of five raccoons of various sizes had been relocated.

For the next few weeks my lawn flourished, and the divots healed. Then, at about 3 a.m. one morning, our dog Dottie bounded off the bed and began barking furiously. The lights on the deck revealed three raccoons, leaning against a wooden chair, grinning.

I went back to making peanut butter sandwiches and carpooling raccoons across town. While releasing my catch one morning, a guy drove up and asked what I was doing. I explained that I lived a few miles away and was trying to move this critter to a safe area.

"We have raccoon problems of our own," he said. "I wish you wouldn't bring yours here." He said he knew of a perfect spot—a place where he'd been releasing his raccoons. As he spoke, it became clear that the area he was describing was about a block from my house.

During all this, the raccoon I had set free a few minutes earlier was clinging to the side of a nearby pine tree.

I'm absolutely certain he was laughing.

13 / OVERDRESSED

"CANDID CAMERA" has always been a low-budget show by Hollywood standards, and a real money-maker by my family's standards. For the specials we produced in the late eighties and early nineties CBS paid a flat fee for each show and allowed us to pocket as much as we could...get away with. We had no studio and no audience. The hosting portions were shot in the field, often at Dad's house. There were no writers, and no scripts. My frustration was that we weren't getting credit for ad-libbing the entire show, because everyone watching naturally assumed we were using a teleprompter. Even CBS was unaware of our process, since Dad's secretary transcribed each program so we could give the network a finished "script."

The Hollywood home-office was perched on a cliff, with a large backyard that stretched down the hillside to a rushing stream. Through seemingly limitless creative energy, my father and his helper, Vladimir Rivera, transformed this acreage into a gorgeous tropical garden, thick with enormous jungle-type plants and trees. The only thing that remained from the previous owners was a sunken hot tub. Whenever I visited from Connecticut I dreaded hearing Dad say, "Why don't we jump in the hot tub before dinner!" He liked to brainstorm about "Candid Camera" gags while soaking.

What could I say? I was his son, his house guest, his employee, and his biggest fan. We'd put on bathing suits and stumble from the house down an always-muddy slope. The hot tub was the kind that you left filled with water—for years, in this case—and, when not in use, covered with a canvas tarp. The canvas on this tub was never properly secured, allowing various things to crawl in. Dad also overlooked adding chemicals to combat whatever was growing in there. Did I mention this was in a jungle? No sun ever hit this spot, and in the evening it was very cold.

After sliding down the hill we'd remove the canvas. What we saw was depicted accurately in the film "National Lampoon's Vacation," when the Griswold family stopped at a motel with a pool that had brown stuff floating in it and was not, well, inviting. Dad's heater was broken, so we were basically sitting in a near-freezing tub of swirling leaves and mud. It's a shame that neither of us did drugs, because any form of chemical assistance would have made the experience more tolerable.

Then there were the tuxedos. Dad believed that one way to counter skimpy production values was to have us wear formal attire on camera—to make our specials seem, for lack of a better word, *special.* This created incongruity that some viewers probably thought was borderline cool, while others thought was nuts. On the "Kitchen Capers" show we wore tuxedos in Dad's kitchen. A "Doctors" show was shot at Norwalk Hospital in Connecticut, with me and co-host Victoria Jackson of "Saturday Night Live" looking like we were going to a prom. More bizarre was our "Sporting Life" special, which opened with me wearing a tux while sinking a putt at the Sterling Farms Golf Course in Stamford, and co-host, "Downtown" Julie Brown, tending the flagstick, dressed as if she were headed to the MTV Awards.

In keeping with our low-budget approach, while Dad did his part of the shows from his Hollywood house, I was working at home in Connecticut. I treated myself to a part-time assistant by placing an ad in the local paper for a job I described as, "part-time assistant." I decided not to mention the words "Candid Camera" or "television" in the ad, since the actual tasks would have little to do with conventional TV and more to do with learning-as-you-go. I wound up hiring a delightful young woman named Dara McDonough, whose regular full-time job, I learned, was responding to police calls of animals being struck on highways. As Dara explained it, if the animal could be saved, she'd bring it to a facility where she and some dedicated colleagues would nurse it. If the animal couldn't be saved, and wasn't already dead, she'd have to euthanize it on the spot. The remains of the animals in the second group were then used to feed those in the first group. What better qualifications could a person possibly have to work on the "Candid Camera" program?

Dara's first assignment involved crawling on the ground at a local golf course, trying to hide strings under mats at the driving range so we could make the ball fall off the tee just as golfers reached the top of their backswings. She was also quite helpful when we set-up a phony "counting room" for an armored car company, where a carefully-aimed room fan was switched on just as unsuspecting bookkeepers were tabulating several thousand dollars in small bills. The bills blew all over the room and Dara and I had to pick them up and stack them neatly for each take.

One day Dara mentioned that she had rescued a baby owl with a broken wing. My thought: We should have appliance repairmen come to a house where the microwave oven was emitting "strange noises." They'd peek inside and see this baby owl, who was perfect for the part because he couldn't fly, was darn cute, and, according to Dara, would actually enjoy being in a dark enclosure—as long as we absolutely, positively made certain there was no electricity running to the device. The gag was effective because it confirmed several things about human nature: (a) "experts" often shoot from the lip, insisting it was a "bad fan motor" before even looking inside; (b) professionals tend to take their work more seriously than those around them do ("It's an animal of some kind! You don't call a service technician when you've got an animal problem!"), and (c) big tough men are very funny when frightened by a tiny owl that's standing on one foot and winking.

Without a doubt the most difficult gag Dara and I pulled off was something I called the *Beaut-o-Matic*. The subjects (unsuspecting people) were professional beauticians who thought they were evaluating a new machine that could do a complete beauty treatment—makeup, hair and nails—in less than 60 seconds. As each of the subjects entered the showroom they met me, playing the sales rep, as well as a young woman named Lisa, who claimed to work at another salon. After describing the wonders of the Beaut-o-Matic, I asked which woman would like to try it, and then I conveniently selected Lisa to go first. She'd remove her shoes and enter the machine, stomach down, on a conveyor belt. After about a minute she came rolling out the other end, with a full "professional makeover." The secret, of course, was that it wasn't Lisa who exited the machine but her identical twin sister, Joanne.

Identical twins are perhaps the best means of convincing people they are seeing something remarkable, which is why magicians so often use twins,

Once both twins were in view, our subject was still unsure what had happened.

yet audiences never seem to catch on. I've done dozens of gags with twins over the years, including an entire twins episode on CBS, and I've never had a subject guess what's up. Once, for example, I wanted to convince airline passengers that their flight had "accidentally" landed back at the airport from which they departed. I used several tricks that day, but the best touch was having a pretty girl say goodbye at the first airport, and her twin sister say hello at the second airport.

In the Beaut-o-Matic gag one beautician, a bubbly blonde in a bright yellow dress, reacted so perfectly it became a Candid Classic (over the years we may have been too liberal in designating sequences as "classics," but this actual seemed to qualify). The woman totally believed that the machine did what I claimed. She examined Joanne's nails and asked, "Can I try it?" After a few more delicious comments, I gave a signal and Lisa rolled out of the machine. Now, with both twins at her side, I told the woman in yellow, "Smile! You're on 'Candid Camera.'" She flipped. But then she exclaimed, "I knew it! I knew it!" Now, that's something we often hear during "reveals." Usually the subject means, "I knew something was unusual here," and not, "I knew this was a television show." In this case, I shot back playfully, "You knew *nothing!*"

And then, as if to prove my point, this delightful woman turned to Lisa, the first twin, and asked, "Did *you* know?"

◆ ◆ ◆

DOING FOUR OR FIVE NETWORK SPECIALS A YEAR is nice work. The pay is good and the grind isn't as bad as weekly-series television. Too bad, then, that things started to go wrong.

The first bit of trouble came in 1989, with the announcement of a new series on the Fox Network, called "Hidden Video," which, according to press reports, was shaping up as a blatant ripoff of "Candid Camera." I got hold of a pilot tape from a New York ad agency and what I saw was puzzling at first and then infuriating. In one sequence, shot at a gas station, a couple was confronted by a roving mariachi band that relentlessly played insipid tunes. Aside from a bad premise and laugh-free execution, the man and woman looked familiar:

They were Barb and Steve North, my college friends from Denver. How's that for coincidence? My old pals, who after college built careers as comedians, were caught in a gag. I phoned Steve and learned that he and Barb had actually been hired to *fake* being caught. The entire Fox show was a fraud.

When Dad saw the tape he went ballistic and immediately filed suit. The case went to binding arbitration, the long and short of which was that Fox: (a) paid our legal fees, (b) fired a low-level producer, (c) changed the name of the show to "Totally Hidden Video" (to *prove* its authenticity), and (d) went on the air as scheduled. Our mistake was not waiting until after the show was broadcast; Fox's deceptive practices would undoubtedly have knocked the series off the air. Instead it lingered for a few years before dying a natural death. But it was a bad omen: Our hidden-camera format was now fair game for others to imitate.

If my father was troubled over Fox's attempt to steal his show, he agonized even more the following year when "Candid Camera" was basically "stolen" again—this time by a company he authorized to do it. King World, the syndication giant responsible for "Wheel of Fortune" and "Jeopardy," wanted to produce a *daily* version of "Candid Camera," to be hosted by Dom DeLuise, the jolly, beret-wearing comic best known for, well, being Dom DeLuise. King World had more cash than it knew what to do with, so it paid Dad $750,000 to basically not be involved with his own show. It reminded me of a scene from the 1978 movie "Heaven Can Wait," in which an eccentric billionaire played by Warren Beatty buys the Los Angeles Rams football team. "He stole my team," says the Rams' owner after closing the deal, "the bastard stole my team."

"How?"

"I demanded five times more than it's worth, and the bastard gave it to me!"

When the King World show hit the air it looked like a cheesy imitation of "Candid Camera," except that it *was* "Candid Camera"—with our theme song, our smiling reveals, and even a few clips from our library. After one season King World was ready to pull the plug but offered to stick with the show for another year if Dad and I were willing to take over as producers and hosts. We might have gone for the new arrangement until we learned that to save money the production would be moved from L.A. to Toronto. It was a frustrating period, made worse by the fact that CBS hated the King World show as much as the public did and stopped buying our specials.

◆ ◆ ◆

WITH "CANDID CAMERA" OUT OF PRODUCTION, I decided to try standup comedy. I had grown comfortable performing in Dad's backyard (where the "audience" consisted of the gardener). Turns out paying customers are much more difficult to please, especially for someone traumatized on stage decades earlier...

I was eight years old, spending a stressful summer away from home in the picturesque Berkshires of Western Massachusetts at Camp Lenox for boys, a place where the sweet smell of pines on the hillside mixed with the odor of kids who resisted taking showers in cold wooden stalls. The highlight—at least for some of the talented campers and their appreciative parents—was the big musical show, which happened to be Gilbert and Sullivan's 1878 comic operetta "H.M.S. Pinafore." The all-male production was cast by the recreation director who, for reasons presumably related to my relatively small size and adolescent vocal range, gave me the role of Buttercup, a female dock merchant. Through standard Gilbert and Sullivan nonsense, Buttercup winds up marrying the ship's captain who has been demoted following the revelation that he was part of a switched-at-birth mixup.

I was so embarrassed that I tried several times to get out of it but wound up having to wear a dress and do the performance. My parents drove 150 miles to witness this atrocity, which had among its low points my wobbly solo in Act One:

> I'm called Little Buttercup, dear Little Buttercup,
> Though I could never tell why.
> But still I'm called Buttercup, poor Little Buttercup,
> Sweet Little Buttercup, I.

So, now it's 1993 and my first paying gig is at a small comedy club attached to a bowling alley in Elmsford, New York. I quickly discover that club patrons: (a) don't really care if you've hosted a bunch of "Candid Camera" specials, (b) believe it's their sworn duty to expose bad material when they hear it, (c) aren't "sweetened" by a laugh track that makes TV performers seem funnier than they are, and (d) confirm what one comedian said: "The drunker they sit there the longer they get." The audience for my 20-minute set consisted of nine people, including Amy. The pay was 50 bucks.

I practiced my act in the shower, the garage, the car—trying to shrink the size of my notes each step of the way. I'd start with a full-size sheet on which I typed out my jokes. Then, I moved to index cards on which I wrote a few phrases. Finally, the day of a performance I'd use tiny bits of paper on which I wrote a word or two representing each joke. One Saturday night in April my note said, "VCR":

"Don't forget Daylight Savings starts tomorrow. That means if your VCR is flashing 12 o'clock all the time, you need to set it to flash 1 o'clock for the next six months."

My big break came at the legendary Pips Comedy Club in Brooklyn, one of the nation's oldest and most renowned comedy venues. Next door was Joe's Clam Bar, where many comics would eat before going on stage. Billy Crystal once noted that if a show didn't go well it was convenient to cross the street and puke into the bay.

My set, while not killer, rose above the vomit level.

Two weeks later I got $125, plus a free hotel room, to do 30 minutes at a club inside a Quality Inn motel. The venue was in the town of . . . wait for it: Lenox, Massachusetts.

Give it up for our next performer, back in the Berkshires after his boffo performance as Buttercup . . .

At least I didn't have to wear a dress.

14 / THREE'S COMPANY

I'VE HOSTED OVER 250 EPISODES of network television and, except for the specials with Dad in his garden, there has always been a "promotable female" at my side. That's Hollywood's indelicate term for a woman who's talented and attractive, naturally, but also has her own fan base and PR platform.

When I took over as host of the CBS specials I had a different partner for every show. There was Audrey Landers from "Dallas," whose mother stood over us every step of the way, like a chaperone at a high school dance. She was followed by another "Dallas" cast member, Morgan Brittany, and then Victoria Jackson of "SNL," who said that her mother had read in the *National Enquirer* that the Funts were "difficult to work with." This quip pretty much guaranteed my best behavior. (I believe the *Enquirer* also said the Funts plotted with aliens to fake the moon landing, so go figure.)

One of my favorites was Leeza Gibbons, who co-hosted our 50th anniversary special on CBS. This was the first show I tried on my own and it was shot on an actual sound stage in Burbank rather than in a garden or some other low-budget location (Morgan Brittany and I did our entire show in a paint store). Ron de Moraes, the two-time Emmy-winning director who stayed with me for 60 shows, suggested, "just have fun with it." Thing is, I was now executive producer and writer as well as host. I was much closer to breaking out in a rash than having fun. Things became even more tense when a bank of lights exploded, showering Leeza and me with glass.

The anniversary show was a hit, giving CBS its first win in the time slot (Thursday, 8 p.m.) in three years. And the reviews were solid: "A hilarious half-century worth of pranks," wrote *People*; "I defy you to keep a straight face through this hour," said *The New York Times*; "Accomplished hosts Peter Funt and Leeza Gibbons are excellent," added *The Hollywood Reporter*.

But you can't please everyone, and clearly displeased was Tom Shales, respected critic for the *Washington Post*. "Allen Funt's ill health would not allow him to host the special," wrote Shales, "so the job goes to his middle-aged son Peter, also the executive producer. Peter may be a bundle of Funt, but he's no bundle of fun. Talk about your glassy-eyed stiffs!"

I always admired the way Tom Shales could turn a phrase, even if he sometimes got carried away doing it. Fact is, I was pretty bad. Before agreeing to more shows, CBS put me through rigorous focus-group testing. They wouldn't show me the questions, which must have been stuff like: "Would you have a beer with this guy?" "Would you have a beer with this guy if he had just confessed to killing your goldfish?" "Would you watch a TV show hosted by a beer-drinking goldfish murderer?"

I presumably passed because CBS bought more specials, allowing me to get better, and after that gave me a weekly series, requiring me to hire more permanent promotable females. I've looked back on every clipping, email and illicit surveillance video, trying to find ways to lampoon the three women I was teamed with after that—and there is nothing. They are the three nicest people I've ever had the pleasure to work with.

That said, I'll do my best to embarrass them . . .

SUZANNE SOMERS

I could probably write a book about Suzanne, but since she's already written a dozen about herself, I'll confine this to a few pages.

For a special called "Battle of the Sexes" CBS execs wanted to pair me with someone vivacious, so they urged me to consider Suzanne, whose sitcom, "Step by Step," was on its last legs—and beautiful legs they were (rim shot). I didn't know much about Suzanne except that she was the blonde in the T-Bird in "American Graffiti," the ditzy character Chrissy Snow on "Three's Company," the mother on "Step by Step"; plus, a movie actress, nightclub performer, lecturer, author, talk show regular and pitch-person for a carload of her own merchandise on shopping channels. One of those products, the ThighMaster, earned her a lot of money and a place in something called (this is true) the *Infomercial Hall of Fame*.

CBS thought a fence might convince our viewers that Suzanne was the girl next door.

Colleagues cautioned me to watch out for Suzanne's husband Alan Hamel. "He's obsessive about every detail in Suzanne's career," they said. "Be careful or soon he'll be producing your show for you."

In negotiating his wife's contract Alan said he and Suzanne would prefer not to be sent to any location that wasn't within a cab ride of a Four Seasons hotel. Plus, I should replace the chairs on our set and fire the lighting director. But I liked Alan, quirks and all.

It was against this background that I went to Beverly Hills to meet Suzanne and shoot her first sequence. Using celebrities in "Candid Camera" gags is often frustrating because many of the skills required in creating a good gag run counter to conventional showbiz training. For one thing, entertainers want to entertain—they assume they must do shtick. A dash of that can be helpful, but the cardinal rule on "Candid Camera" is: When the subject is reacting, be quiet. Then there's the recognition thing. Celebrities expect to be recognized when they're out in public, yet Dad and I both discovered that a simple disguise—such as a hat and glasses—is all that's needed to fool folks.

Many stars can't handle this; they've spent an entire career seeking recognition yet here they are being mistaken for a waitress or gas station attendant. The safest approach is allowing the celebrity to play his or her self. Recognition is no longer an issue, and much of the dialogue relies on simply saying what comes naturally. I created a gag in which Suzanne would be herself, doing an in-store appearance to promote a perfume called *Somers' Night*. She'd invite customers to sample its fragrance, and the joke was, it had none. It was odorless tap water.

Suzanne was to be dropped off at one o'clock. As I later discovered, she is never dropped off; Alan drives her to work, hangs around, and drives her home. That was fine with me—no limos. And she does her own hair and makeup. Wow! Suzanne is the girl next-door—only a lot richer, curvier, and has been on the covers of both *Playboy* and *Alternative Medicine Digest*.

They were parked at the curb on Rodeo Drive in some sort of over-sized passenger van. I guess it was a maxi minivan. "Come on in," she said. And now I'm hunched over in the back of this van, trying to explain things like, "don't talk when the subjects are talking" and "don't block the subjects' light" and "be sure to work the microphone so it's always pointed in the subjects' direction."

There are psychological tricks in doing our sequences. In the no-smell perfume gag we were looking for humorous examples of how the power of suggestion can make people really believe they smell something, even if they can't. Thus, you wouldn't want to say, "Try this. It's very subtle." It would be better to say, "Try this. Some people tell me it's too *strong*." If the subject says, "I don't smell anything," don't give up. Ask, "Well, which is more potent, the lemon or the lavender?"

Suzanne did her best to absorb all of this, but she had difficulty giving it an edge. After a good opening minute or two, she'd let subjects off the hook. Still, I felt we had a solid sequence, so you can imagine my disappointment when I saw Suzanne's promotional appearance on the syndicated talk show "Live with Regis & Kathie Lee":

REGIS: *Were you a part of any of the stunts?*
SUZANNE: *I was. I was a part of a stunt. I'm not a good stunt person.*
KATHIE LEE: *You're too recognizable.*
SUZANNE: *No, it's not really that. I went as myself. I was having a new perfume called Somers' Night, and I was bringing people in off the street and asking, "What do you think of it?" And it was water. And I kept saying, "Do you smell the rosemary or the lavender?" But I would feel sorry for them. I didn't want them to look stupid, and I'd go, "Well, it's subtle. Yeah, it's real, real subtle. I wouldn't be surprised if you couldn't smell it." And Peter Funt's coming out and going, "You're wrecking the spot." And I go, "Yeah, I know, but I just can't do it."*
REGIS: *You don't have the heart.*

I had to count to one hundred before calling the Four Seasons Hotel to tell Alan what I thought about Suzanne's "plug" for our show. I pointed out that while honesty is a good policy, her mission was promotional and she wasn't exactly being grilled by Mike Wallace.

Maybe we got the sympathy vote. As soon as record ratings came out for "Battle of the Sexes" CBS offered me a weekly series. This time there would be no arguing about possible co-hosts. Suzanne had proved to be a valuable asset for the special and I was eager to have her as a partner on the series. Alan Hamel didn't haggle much about Suzanne's new contract, except for a new wrinkle about wardrobe.

For all of her Chrissy-ness, Suzanne is no dummy. She knew that "Candid Camera" was my baby. I created the gags, organized the show, and wrote the words each of us spoke. She might easily be looked upon as window dressing. Well, someone once said—perhaps it was Alan Hamel—if you're going to be window dressing, you'd better provide a helluva view. Alan prevailed upon us to employ his daughter, Leslie Hamel, to design outfits for Suzanne to wear on each show. The clothes would belong to Suzanne, not our production company, and we would pay $5,000 for each weekly creation. In the overall scheme of things—remember, Suzanne did her own hair and makeup—it seemed acceptable. I never dreamed that these outfits would create a major fuss among viewers, the network, and even my own staff and family.

Leslie's first dress was bright orange, covered with what must have been a zillion little mirrors, each reflecting enough light to make viewers wish they were wearing sunglasses. As to its length, when Suzanne was standing it really wasn't bad. But for some reason when she sat down it looked as if she was wearing a top and no bottom. I walked on stage and blurted, "Whoa! Now that's what I call a dress!" Suzanne lapped it up. "Oh, this old thing?" she cooed. The next week she appeared in a tuxedo-style top with black hot pants and I told the audience, "My partner's serving drinks after the show." One night I had on a brown suit and Suzanne appeared in a vibrant purple number. I said, "We look like a peanut butter and jelly sandwich."

On the Christmas show she was dressed entirely in bridal white with a bouquet of live flowers the size of a football on her head. "Don't worry," I said as we greeted viewers, "I've got two guys ready to water your head during commercials."

Before long everyone had an opinion about Suzanne's wardrobe. CBS asked me to have her tone it down. Viewers somehow developed the notion that I was forcing her to wear certain styles. Others insisted that my ad-libs were demeaning. They didn't realize that Suzanne loves cracks about her appearance.

Clothing fixations notwithstanding, our show was a hit and Suzanne and I were having great fun. She worked to ensure that viewers got a positive impression, for example insisting we hold hands whenever we walked on or off stage. When we were seated, she would always cross her left leg over her right so that her foot would be pointed *at* me and not away; she felt certain that if her foot pointed away from me viewers would believe we were feuding or unhappy with each other.

One time Suzanne flubbed a line and we had to stop tape. For the benefit of the studio audience she quipped, "When you hired me you never said I had to read!" To which I replied, "It was so dark in the room, who would ever think about reading?"

DINA EASTWOOD

After four seasons, CBS chief Les Moonves made an unusual offer: "Candid Camera" could stay on CBS, but we'd go back to quarterly specials rather than a weekly series. It was sort of like the gag we did in a hotel where arriving guests were told they had been *downgraded* to a smaller room.

I talked to other outlets and was intrigued by what I heard from a former CBS president, Jeff Sagansky, who had taken the top job at the PAX cable channel, partly owned by NBC. If we produced new weekly episodes of "Candid Camera" on PAX, we could repurpose the best sequences to create periodic specials on NBC—the best of both worlds. I signed with Jeff and, almost immediately, NBC and PAX began feuding. Worse, the NBC entertainment president, Jeff Zucker, made a regrettable move: he bought a rip-off hidden-camera show called "Spy TV," a series that Entertainment Weekly called "'Candid Camera' for sadomasochists." Then insult was heaped upon injury. Jeff Sagansky phoned with NBC's new idea: "Zucker wonders if you'd be interested in a summer slot on NBC, immediately following 'Spy TV.'"

Say what? Package "Candid Camera" with its competitor?

"Zucker says if you think 'Spy TV' is that bad, why not come on right after it? What better way to show viewers the difference between the shows?"

I said no. But that left me producing "Candid Camera" for PAX with a much lower budget than I had at CBS and without hope of getting supplemental revenue from NBC. And, the PAX episodes would be full hours: double the content for half the price. I was doing what's known as *deficit financing*—a technical term meaning "losing money."

Cuts were needed, starting with Suzanne and her custom-made outfits. To replace Suzanne I had to find a talented co-host who could handle the assignment and also generate publicity for the show, while working for much less pay—an up-and-comer, a woman with more in the way of *potential* than actual TV credits. As it turned out, I didn't have to look far. Dina Ruiz lived about a mile from me in Pebble Beach, and her married name was as well known as any in show business.

I'd been friends with Dina ever since I moved to California. She was a news anchor on the local NBC station and a dedicated volunteer for several Monterey County charities. We often sat together at fund-raising dinners. It was at one such event that she first told me in a whisper that she had gone on a date with Clint Eastwood, 35 years her senior. Dina married Clint in Las Vegas in 1996.

She was thrilled for a chance to co-host "Candid Camera." Although she was using her maiden name at KSBW, I insisted that with us she'd have to be known as Dina Eastwood. She immediately understood that a famous last name would get attention. After all, if it weren't for my last name I wouldn't be hosting "Candid Camera" either.

Arriving in Hollywood with Clint aboard the Time-Warner jet, Dina was visibly nervous. The gig wasn't a local newscast or a Rotary Club luncheon. We had long talks about what, exactly, she should try to be. One thing was certain: she shouldn't try to be Suzanne Somers. But being Dina Ruiz from KSBW wouldn't exactly cut it either. We needed wholesome but not boring. Stylish but not too sexy. Funny but not nutty. Dina was more comfortable doing field sequences than Suzanne had been. Conversely, Dina didn't shine in the studio with quite the same wattage Suzanne possessed. But "Candid Camera" is all about gags in the field, and I tried to come up with as many sequences for Dina as I could.

At a roadside diner in Texas she played a waitress who tasted the customers' food. At a dry cleaning shop in California she played a clerk who happened to be wearing the customers' clothes. In Wisconsin Dina was an elevator operator who refused to leave the ground floor until she had five passengers—"to save energy." In Arizona she played a clerk who insisted on charging for "shipping and handling," even when customers bought small items such as gum or candy. And in my favorite, shot in California, Dina portrayed a traffic cop who wrote tickets to people for parking "illegally" in their own driveways.

Unlike Alan Hamel, who camped out at our studio whenever Suzanne was working, Clint rarely visited. I recall seeing him once, standing in the shadows backstage, seeming uncertain about how he should act while his wife was working, and desperately afraid that someone would ask him something. I offered him a snack from our craft-service food table. "Thanks," he said, "but I've got people waiting." And he left for another five months.

Whenever I see Clint I flash back to the first time he gave me, Amy and our kids a ride to L.A. on the Warner Bros. jet. We had already buckled our seatbelts and were ready for takeoff, when Clint lumbered down the aisle carrying a *pig*.

It was a Vietnamese potbelly pig named Penelope. I learned it was the latest animal member of the Eastwood household, joining chickens, rats and other creatures. "We couldn't leave her home alone," explained Dina, failing to mention that "alone" in this particular case meant in the company of housekeepers, gardeners and relatives, just not an actual Eastwood. "Besides," she added, "Clint's become very attached to Penelope; she spent last night with us in our bed."

So here we have one of the richest, most powerful men in show business, sitting in a multi-zillion-dollar jet, eating a gourmet vegetable wrap with one hand, reading the Carmel Pine Cone newspaper propped on the table in front of him, and, with his other hand, cuddling a pig. Be sure to conjure that image if you ever find yourself thinking you've seen it all.

MAYIM BIALIK

In 2014 I needed a new partner for a limited run of "Candid Camera" on TV Land ("limited" is an industry term meaning we asked for 20 hours and they gave us 10).

My partner Ben Silverman—the former NBC boss and accomplished Hollywood dealmaker—mentioned that Mayim Bialik might be willing to take the job. He said "might" because Mayim was in the cast of television's number one comedy series, "The Big Bang Theory," and presumably didn't have time or interest to *watch* TV Land let alone work on one of its shows. But Ben used to date Mayim's manager, Tiffany Kuzon, so he was engaging in a bit of insider trading when he arranged for Tiffany, Mayim, and my agent Mark Itkin to meet with Ben and me at the Yen Sushi restaurant in Burbank.

Ben and Tiffany sat across from each other and spoke in ex-lovers' code about shared memories; Mayim and I sat across from each other and talked nonstop for an hour the way people do when they're exploring each other's brains, and Mark sat quietly eating sushi. Mayim didn't look like a typical Hollywood actress. She had on little or no makeup and her unfussy style was refreshingly down to earth. Mayim has a Ph.D. in neuroscience from UCLA, for which her dissertation was titled "Hypothalamic regulation in relation to maladaptive, obsessive-compulsive, affiliative and satiety behaviors in Prader-Willi syndrome." She also knows her way around showbiz, having played numerous film and TV roles beginning at age 11, and starring in her own NBC sitcom, "Blossom," at age 14. By the time Mark finished his sushi, Mayim was onboard.

Mayim is an intriguing combination of brains, beauty (inner and outer) and... social media. I wouldn't have pegged her as the My-Life-Is-an-Open-Instagram-Post type. But Mayim is relentless in posting things like "Here I am arriving at the studio!" or "Which outfit should I wear on today's show?!" and "Doesn't Peter look handsome doing the audience warm-up?"*

* Used for illustration only; I don't know if Mayim actually posted that.

Mayim's YouTube channel has over a million devoted subscribers who enjoy hearing her takes on "What PMS Is Really Like" and "6 Breastfeeding Tips for New Moms" and "Remembering My Wedding After Divorce." Plus: "My Son Teaches Me Tik Tok Dances."

About our show, *The New York Times* critic wrote:

"...the reboot of "Candid Camera" that TV Land broadcast ... was an update of the Allen Funt show from the early days of television, but more or less as gentle as the initial years of the original series were. A waitress samples the food of startled restaurant guests. Residents of Queens are brought new recycling bins: eight full-size trash cans, each a different color. (Brown: poultry waste. Violet: toxic waste.) Peter Funt (Allen's son) and Mayim Bialik of "The Big Bang Theory" paired rather well to sell the good-natured, hostility-free clips."

The ratings were strong by TV Land's standards, prompting the head of programming to email: "Holy sh$t!"

And that was pretty much my reaction when TV Land fired its top executives, revamped its lineup and, as TV people put it, "Went in a different direction."

A viewer created this spitting image of Mayim and me.

15 / CAKEWALK

MANY VIEWERS—and most network executives—don't really understand what makes a good "Candid Camera" gag. The easiest suggestions to toss aside are those that begin, "You should catch my uncle, he's really funny." I think the idea we've received most is: "Have someone come out of a restroom with a long piece of toilet paper attached to their shoe!" (People think an exclamation point makes an idea better. "Rig an ATM so it gives Monopoly money!")

Our gags can be grouped by type:

REVERSAL: Our actress drives into a gas station and asks the attendant to *remove* five gallons. A charity asks people how much they'd be willing to *receive.*

TEMPTATION: When we left a tray of goodies in a supermarket with the sign, "Free—One to a Customer," most people took three or four, and one guy took the tray.

AUTHORITARIAN: Our actor stopped motorists on a quiet road leading into Delaware. "Sorry," he said. "Delaware is closed today." Few people argued; most just turned around. Our guy added, "You might try New Jersey, it's open."

GROUP PRESSURE: The most memorable piece—used in college classes and corporate training sessions—is titled "Face the Rear." Three "Candid Camera" staffers enter an elevator along with one unsuspecting subject. On a silent cue the "Candid" confederates turn and face the rear of the car. Invariably, the subject turns as well. When the group turns back, so does the subject.

LINGUISTIC: "I wouldn't go in there," Dad once told a guy entering a drug store, "these people are very retroactive." Another time he asked a man, "Where can I buy some scruples?" The guy thought about it and answered, "I haven't seen any since I was a kid."

FINANCIAL: I posed as a bank teller selling counterfeit money. I was a clerk giving change in yen because "Japan is our country of the day." I played a Samaritan collecting funds in Arizona to save the Grand Canyon. ("We're not certain what we're saving it from, but we want to be ready.")

BUREAUCRATIC: At a government office we told people they'd have to change their last name because the new census indicated their current name was overused. A post office allowed us to sell "0-cent stamps." ("They show support for our mail carriers.")

COMMERCIAL: We held a "99-Cent Sale" in which everything on sale was 99 cents, including many items that on other days were, say, a dime. We baffled customers with a great sale on women's clothing: "110% OFF."

PSYCHOLOGICAL: In a wine tasting, participants didn't know every glass was poured from the same bottle—so they gave each a different score. At a gym, people inhaling "pure oxygen" felt a rush of energy—not realizing what they got was ordinary room air.

MECHANICAL: When it's Man Against Machine, always bet on the machine. That's true whether it's a self-serve ice cream machine that won't stop serving, or a restroom dryer that squirts a fine mist so hands never get dry.

COGNITIVE DISSONANCE: We made a building disappear. We had a parachutist plunge through the ceiling. And we built an elevator that went sideways.

OBSERVATIONAL: This is certainly the most fundamental form of "Candid Camera." We've watched how people walk on stairs, how kids brush their teeth, how teens comb their hair, and how people put in contact lenses for the first time.

Some ideas defy categorization. I asked prop guy Don Laurino to rig a large seashell so it played music. (You know, if you hold a shell to your ear you can supposedly hear the ocean. So why not Hawaiian music?)

I sent Linda Gulley to tell people the local newspaper was recalling copies that had been delivered a few hours earlier. "This edition is just filled with mistakes," she said.

I told Dick Briglia to find a vet in New York who would tell dog owners that their pet's teeth needed braces. Dick called back to report, "No good. It seems half the vets in Manhattan actually make orthodontics for dogs." (We changed the gag to glasses for dogs, and it was very funny.)

◆ ◆ ◆

OUT OF NEARLY A MILLION PEOPLE photographed by "Candid Camera" only one has the distinction of being caught in a sequence and then, nearly four decades later, turning the tables to catch other unsuspecting people in the very same gag. It's Richard Lewis, the comedian who fashioned a career in stand-up, TV and film by cashing in on his neuroses. The titles of his various cable specials probably paint him best: "I'm Exhausted," "I'm in Pain," and, of course, the "Magical Misery Tour." His acclaimed memoir was called, "The OTHER Great Depression." Richard was born three months before I was, which means he, too, has a lifespan that mirrors the "Candid Camera" show.

When he was 15, attending Dwight Morrow High School in Englewood, New Jersey, Richard was called to the guidance counselor's office to hear the results of a standardized aptitude test. He sat there with a smug expression, looking rather preppy with neatly combed thick black hair and a dark sweater over a white shirt and tightly knotted tie. He didn't know "Candid Camera" was at the school that day, or that the counselor was helping to catch students in a gag.

"I've come to the very definite and firm conclusion," said the counselor, "that you would be perfectly suited for manual labor." Richard's eyes bulged as the camera zoomed in. "Did you say manual labor?" he asked, knowing he couldn't possibly have given any answers on the exam to suggest he intended to work for a living.

"Yes."

"That's all, just manual labor? Gee, I never thought I was suited for manual labor. You mean no intelligence? Just manual labor?" He kept saying "manual labor" as if by repeating it enough it might take on new meaning.

The counselor left the room and another student joined Richard. "He says I'm suited for manual labor! What does he think, I'll be a bricklayer or something? I felt like punching him."

Of course, even if the test had been legitimate it's not likely the results would have identified a career as "stand-up comic." But after Richard Lewis became *Richard Lewis*, he told me repeatedly how much he enjoyed the gag. "I had aspirations of becoming some kind of writer," he recalled. "I just felt manual labor was not my gig, you know, so I was freaked out." Richard and I decided to visit a high school in California and have him play the guidance counselor, doing the same gag.

He still had that thick black hair, but now it was in a ponytail. And he wore heavy glasses that fit the counselor role. "I've come to the firm conclusion," he told a teenage girl, "that after you finish school it would be best for you to focus on a career in the circus."

"The circus?" she said, with an expression very much like the one Richard had years earlier.

"Are you surprised? Am I the first person to tell you that?" Richard was rolling now. "Do you have any circus acts in your family? Any relatives who ran away with the circus?"

"No," replied the girl, stuck midway between surprise and tears. "I'd be the first."

As the day went on, Richard told one young man he'd have a great career playing badminton. He informed a girl that she should seek a job in "waste disposal," particularly *toxic waste*.

Then, there was a serious-looking boy who explained, "I really wanted to pursue something in math..."

"I see," said Richard. "So, designing slippers and footwear is something that's a shock to you?"

The irony in the Richard Lewis story is that even though his "aptitude test" in 1964 was a fake, being on "Candid Camera" actually put him on a career path that he would follow for the rest of his life. "I was hooked," he said. "I got the bug that day and never looked back."

In 1990 I happened to catch another funny guy, who also went on to have a very successful career in stand-up comedy and TV. Jeff Foxworthy was already in the early stages of fame—but not very far along—when I knocked on his hotel room door in Stamford, Connecticut, dressed as a bellman. We

Richard Lewis gave students quite an education.

were doing a special about "Signs" so we had the hotel print an exact copy of its regular DO NOT DISTURB sign, except it said, PLEASE DISTURB. I picked rooms at random and placed our sign on doors, then tried to create as big a disturbance as possible. Things were going well, although it was a tough assignment for cameraman Ira Speir because the only way we could shoot this gag was to put Ira and his equipment on a bellman's cart, cover him with laundry, and then roll him down the corridor and park in front of each door where I'd do the bit.

Jeff Foxworthy was still three years away from developing his "You Might Be a Redneck If..." routine which came out in book form in 1993, selling 14 million copies and leading to a dozen other books and numerous TV appearances. ("You might be a redneck if you think the last words to The Star Spangled Banner are 'gentlemen start your engines.'" "You might be a redneck if your high school basketball game got rained out.") He answered his hotel room door barefoot, wearing jeans but no shirt.

"Hi," I said. "Was there some form that you wanted the disturbance to take?"

"I'm sorry?" he replied, rubbing his eyes.

"Did you get your disturbance yet?"

"I don't know what you're talking about."

"The hotel disturbance, did you get it yet?"

"I have no idea what you're talking about."

Jeff was a good subject: puzzled, even a bit miffed, but not angry. I pulled out a horn, the type circus clowns use, and gave him a blast. "Does that work for you?" I asked.

"That works."

I pointed to the sign on his door, and he sort of started to get it, without really getting it. In other words, Jeff knew something was up, but he had no idea it was "Candid Camera." He went into stand-up mode:

"Can you come back in the morning?" he asked. "Come at four or five o'clock tomorrow morning. You don't have any fireworks do you?"

I allowed him to close the door. Then, I knocked again and said, "We never like people on 'Candid Camera' to kid us more than we kid them."

"You know who you've got here?" he asked in a CIA-type whisper.

"I don't have the faintest idea."

"I'm a comedian," he said, still whispering. "I'm working in town."

"Well, give yourself a plug. What's your name?"

"Jeff Foxworthy," he answered in a much louder voice.

The next day I sent the tape to my father's office in Hollywood for editing. We had many funny subjects to choose from, and none of us had ever heard of Jeff Foxworthy, so I wasn't surprised when Jeff's clip was left out of the final version that ran on CBS. Fourteen years later, Bill Cartwright called me into his editing room. (It was Bill, you may recall, who made the discovery that baseball pitcher Andy Pettitte had been caught *in the act of being himself* on "Candid Camera.") "Are you aware that we've got Jeff Foxworthy in the outtakes from this old sequence?" Bill asked.

"*The* Jeff Foxworthy?"

"Yeah, the redneck guy."

We ran Jeff's piece the following week. Since he was not actually hired to be on our show, he wasn't paid for his appearance. But I learned that Jeff works with the Duke University Children's Hospital in North Carolina, where they specialize in treating kids with cancer. So we invented a $5,000 fee, and donated it to the hospital in Jeff's name.

Jeff Foxworthy was caught by "Candid Camera" before he was a star simply because I happened to knock on his door; Richard Lewis was caught the same way—right place, right time. That's quite different than planning to trick celebrities, which is something I don't enjoy. When caught, their minds flash to how they looked without makeup, whether they were funny or said something dirty. And what if their agent steps in and demands an exorbitant fee? It's a mess, and it makes me suspicious of shows that claim to catch celebrities. One actress who appeared on Dick Clark's "Bloopers and Practical Jokes" told me that after the "reveal" she was asked to reshoot the ending so she could act more surprised. That's something we'd never do.

ON A FEW OCCASIONS I have been asked (commanded, really) to catch established performers in a gag. It helps keep the network happy and, in the case of two reporters from "Entertainment Tonight," it can turn out to be pretty funny.

Much as "Candid Camera" pioneered reality TV, "ET" was a breakthrough program in showbiz reporting. I have several connections to "ET," going back to the early eighties when I was assigned by *The New York Times* to write about Al Masini, the maverick ad sales executive who invented the show. Beyond recognizing the market for celebrity news, Masini's breakthrough came when he helped raise $22 million to finance the installation of satellite-receiving dishes at more than 100 local TV stations, so "ET's" reports could be fresh each day. Two of "ET's" popular hosts, Mary Hart and Leeza Gibbons, have participated in Candid Camera shows over the years, and for several seasons director Ron de Moraes did both our show and "ET." With all that history, you'd think we could get a free plug on "ET" but the competition for its airtime is intense, so I found myself trying to invent a gag that would essentially force them to publicize what we were doing, because it would be all about them. With the help of "ET's" executive producer, Linda Bell Blue, I arranged to catch two of her top reporters, Jann Carl and Chris Wragge.

In planning gags, especially those focused on high-level professionals, I try to find the inherent points of frustration in their particular line of work, and then exaggerate them. For TV reporters assigned to interview celebrities there are two frequent pitfalls: an overly-demanding star who sets unreasonable ground rules, and a press agent or publicist who treats the reporter like a pawn in a PR campaign. "ET" sent Chris to interview Dolly Parton and Jann to interview Clint Eastwood at a fancy hotel suite in Santa Monica. I played the publicist, and I had the makeup people dye my hair black and give me a mustache and glasses (I looked sort of like the late Sonny Bono on a bad day).

Chris arrived first, and I explained that Dolly was in the next room getting dressed but that I would be happy to "go over any questions" that he would be asking.

"I thought we'd talk about her theme park," said Chris, "and her new album, plans for a TV show, and, you know, what it's like being a sex symbol."

"We're not doing that anymore," I said, jumping in. "We're trying to step back from the sex symbol thing, so work with me on that."

"Anything else?" asked Chris.

"Did they mention the jams and jellies?"

"No."

"Dolly's got her own line of Down-Home Jams and Jellies, and that's why we're here, to promote the jams and jellies."

Chris looked concerned. He had tolerated this obnoxious PR guy, but he can't limit his interview with Dolly Parton to, of all things, *jelly*.

The phone rang. "Yes, honey, are you almost ready?" I said. "Yes, the guy is here." (Turning to Chris): "Your name is..."

"Chris."

"It's Chris, Dolly. It's going to be a fellow named Chris. What? Hold on."

(To Chris): "Is Mary Hart going to come to do the actual interview?"

"No. I'm doing the actual interview."

"Yourself?"

"Yes, I'm the interviewer."

"Dolly, Mary's not coming. It's a gentleman named..."

"Chris."

"Chris somebody..."

"Chris Wragge."

"Chris Wragge." (To Chris): "What have you done, Chris? Have you interviewed people before?"

Now he looked even more bummed. "I've interviewed everyone from John Travolta to Kurt Russell to Bette Middler. Hundreds of people."

As Chris shifted in his seat, I decided to turn the screws by saying another TV show was expected shortly. "I thought with you we'd just talk about the jams and jellies," I explained. "And then with this other show we'd do the music thing and she'd sing a little."

"Do you understand what show we're from?"

"Yes, 'Entertainment Tonight.'"

At this point my assistant came in to report, "Dolly is having a zipper problem but she'll be ready soon."

"Listen, Chris," I continued. "Pretend I was Dolly. Ask me the questions you have in mind about jams and jellies."

"Let me tell you something. I don't mean to be rude, but I've been doing this for eight years now, and I've never in my life..." He interrupted himself, caught his breath and continued. "I'm not going to sit here and discuss my line of questions. I'm very conversational; I'm not here to squeeze anyone; I'm not going to rake anyone over the coals. But I don't need this crap. The reason they sent me here is because I'm the feel-good guy of the show."

"The what?"

"The feel-good guy. I make everyone feel relaxed. I'm not here to ask difficult questions, this is a patsy interview..."

"Don't' say patsy when she comes out," I interjected, referring to the legendary Patsy Cline, although I don't think Chris caught my drift.

"No, I'd never say that."

"Well, you just did. Now listen, will you hold up the jams and jellies while you interview her?"

"Probably not, because this isn't an infomercial."

"Do you want to hold up the raspberry, the strawberry or the peach?"

"It wouldn't make any difference whatsoever."

"But she's going to ask you if you eat it all the time and what's your favorite flavor."

"I'd probably go with the raspberry."

As my talk with Chris continued I was getting that rush that comes with an overwhelming success. But just then he jumped up and left the room to rant to his director. I whispered to my crew that I was afraid the best stuff was now going to happen down the hall. He finally returned, bringing the director along. I figured it was time for the reveal.

"Can you smile Chris?" I asked.

"On occasion."

"You're on 'Candid Camera.'"

"You're kidding! You jerks! I've been had!"

I learned from my friends at "ET" that Chris Wragge caught a lot of flak in the weeks that followed for having declared himself the "feel-good guy." He left "ET" a few months later and pursued a career as a television sports reporter and then news anchor. He married a former Playboy Playmate of the Year, Victoria Silvstedt who, in an unrelated twist of fate, was featured in a "Candid Camera" episode a few weeks after Chris's appearance. We hired Victoria to play the part of a gas station attendant—typecasting never having been one of my concerns—at the "full service" pump, where motorists expect to get their windshields washed and oil checked in return for paying more for gas. Victoria claimed her nail polish was wet and basically enticed male customers to check their own oil and wash their windows; she even had them pump their own gas. Looking back, the only thing I care to say about her work on "Candid Camera" is that she's the only performer in the history of our show to be bleeped more than the unsuspecting subjects.

Following Chris Wragge into the hotel suite was Jann Carl, who had a long career with "ET" and occasionally subbed for Mary Hart as anchor. Jann believed she was going to interview Clint Eastwood about his new "artichoke business." She mentioned that Paul Newman had a well-known line of pop-corn and other food products, so I cautioned her never to mention Newman when talking to Clint. "Gosh," she said, "I had no idea Clint was so sensitive."

Jann's reactions were amusingly similar to those we got from Chris but when we reached the reveal she burst into, "I knew it! I knew it!" just like the woman who was caught in the *Beaut-o-Matic* gag. And just like the woman who believed a machine could do a makeover in less than a minute, Jann really knew nothing—in fact she had a difficult time finding the camera even after I told her where it was.

◆ ◆ ◆

HAVING JANN AND CHRIS on "Candid Camera" was terrific promotion for us as well as for "ET," which ran our footage plus interviews. Mary Hart even did the famous "Smile! You're on Candid Camera!" tag line at the end of our pro-gram. So it was difficult for me to say "no" when a CBS executive called with word that, "We were wondering…" if you could do a gag to catch figure skater Tara Lipinski, the Olympic gold medal winner, to promote her upcoming CBS special. It was so difficult for me to say "no" that all I managed to say was, "yes." In hindsight, I probably should have said, "where?" since the location turned out to be Lake Placid, New York—several hundreds miles north of no-where. It was in Lake Placid's former Olympic Village that Tara and a troupe of skaters, led by Scott Hamilton, were rehearsing for the CBS show. And perhaps I should have said, "huh?" when Hamilton told me that we should do a gag about balloons because, "Tara's really scared of balloons." Instead, I believe my exact words were, "Yeah, sure."

So here we were on a cross-country jaunt to a town where the hotels didn't even get CNN, freezing our lens caps off, hoping that one try with a sweet little figure skater, who's frightened of balloons, would somehow yield something funny.

I'm going to interrupt myself, because like many travelers I Googled "Lake Placid" and came across a batch of Yahoo! "User Reviews."

Here, unaltered, is the first entry I found:

"I took a chance on Lake Placid because I didn't have any money to go to Miami Beach, Virginia Beach, London or the Carribean. It was a five hour peaceful drive up the I87 with my fiance, a well needed time to conversate and reflect on us. We stayed at an affordable Inn, called The Pines of Lake Placid. Nothing fancy, but all we really needed was a Bed and a Bathroom. We toured Main Street which had some great shopping, Gap outlet, Van Heusen, and Jeffrey Beane. There was also a restaurant called GoldBerries which had the most delicious Omlettes I have ever tasted. The view of the lake was breath taking and the walk around the lake was some good excercise. Me and my fiancee also visited the Verizon Sports complex where we did our first Bob Sled ride, it was auxilarating. Lake Placid is known for winter Sports, we visited in the summer and we still had loads of fun. And Oh Yeah you've gotta take a ride down Ausable Chasm."

All I can say about that report is that it's a lot funnier than anything I accomplished in Lake Placid involving balloons, but I'm getting ahead of myself. I decided to use the old "publicity photo" gag that had worked for us so many times. Tara would pose in front of several dozen balloons, which were rigged to pop. Actually, "rigged" is a professional term implying care and attention, or at least the spending of considerable sums of money. What we had was Tara standing in front of a curtain, and Don Laurino hiding behind the curtain with a pin. Dick Briglia played the photographer and I played a guy who happened to be standing with the photographer. Here, with Dick's comments removed, is the transcript of every word that Tara Lapinski said during the "Balloon Gag," as broadcast on the CBS Television Network:

TARA: *[First balloon pops. Second balloon pops. Third balloon pops.] Oh my God!*
TARA: *[Fourth balloon pops.] Aahhh!*
ME: *What's going on? Are you allergic to balloons?*
TARA: *No.*

ME: *Tara, do you know me? I'm Peter Funt from the 'Candid Camera'* *show. We popped all these balloons just to see how you'd react. And you're as* *sweet with balloons as you are on the ice. [Fifth balloon pops.]*

TARA: *Oh!*

The next morning my crew and I flew back to California. For our show, Suzanne Somers interviewed Tara about her experience:

SUZANNE: *What did you think when those balloons started popping?*

TARA: *I had no idea what was going on. And by, like, the third time it* *popped, I was like, maybe we shouldn't use balloons for this photo shoot.*

A few days after the broadcast, I received the following letter from Tara's agent, Michael Burg:

On behalf of Tara, her mom and myself, I just want to say thanks for *lending your time recently in Lake Placid. I think we all agree the best* *stunt was when we surprised Tara with the balloons.*

From this I learned: (a) It doesn't take much to please a network, a performer or an agent when all they're after is publicity; (b) Tara Lapinski is, indeed, scared of balloons—but she's very nice about it; (c) It would be a warm day in Lake Placid before we did another gag like that; and, (d) Regardless of my opinion, some people apparently find Lake Placid, New York, quite auxilarating.

♦ ♦ ♦

BASED ON SUCH EXPERIENCES I tensed up whenever CBS *suggested* we have one of its performers appear in a gag. The worst example came in the late nineties when the network was trying to promote a failing beauty pageant operated by Donald Trump and it seemed—at least to CBS vice presidents— that Trump would be funny in one of our stunts. This proved to be almost as bad a judgment as the one voters would make in 2016.

Trump was between wives at the time, so I came up with a gag in which professional matchmakers were called to Trump Tower, where Trump explained that he needed a date. He claimed he wanted a woman in keeping with his new image, "really down to earth." As Trump spoke we sent in flashy women from his staff for Trump to flirt with. He then told each matchmaker, "That's what I mean, someone wholesome and simple like her."

Trump was good at leering but refused our advice about what to say to make the bit funny. After a few hours we decided he was too lame for CBS. (Though years later we salvaged some of it for cable, we basically had to tell Trump: You're fired.)

Trump loved the leering but he never understood the joke's irony.

◆ ◆ ◆

ANOTHER TIME a CBS vice president asked me to catch some of the network's stars. He had in mind Christine Lahti, the Emmy- and Oscar-winning actress starring at the time in the dramatic series "Chicago Hope"; the tightly-wound actress Cybill Shepherd, whose sitcom "Cybill" was struggling and in need of promotion, and the comic Ray Romano, star of CBS's hit sitcom "Everybody Loves Raymond."

I needed a gag that would be what magicians call a self-worker—that is, a gag in which whatever happens is per se entertaining. CBS was celebrating its corporate birthday, so I thought...huge cake...cake falls over on cue... big, quick laugh. We'd tell the celebrities that CBS wanted a publicity photo of them blowing out the candles. I rented a large mobile home and set it up as a portable photographic studio that we could drive to each location where the CBS stars were working. We got a supply of multi-tiered cakes, decorated with "Happy Birthday CBS," and rigged an invisible fishing line so that one of our guys could make the cake topple over at the right moment. I posed as an obnoxious art director, and an actual CBS photographer, Cliff Lipson, pretended to take the still photo while we shot the "Candid" video.

As Christine Lahti walked toward our trailer outside the "Chicago Hope" studio, the head of CBS's photo department whispered in my ear, "Be careful. I don't think she's very happy with us right now. She walked out in the middle of a publicity shoot last week because we were taking too long." (Did I mention that I hate tricking celebrities?)

Since my goal was to create some humorous anxiety, I told Christine the cake cost over $400 and that she should be careful not to bump the little table on which it sat. I called her "Katherine" and, with an arrogant edge, said I had never seen her show.

In fairness, I'd like to state that I don't believe I could handle such provocation without blowing my top. I'm capable of losing it when a restaurant doesn't get my order right. Yet, here I was pretending to work for CBS, insulting this wonderful actress by getting her name wrong.

She blew out the candle, Russ Simon pulled the string from his hiding place, and much to my delight the four-tiered cake fell over perfectly.

"Did you bump the table?" I asked.

"No!" she said, clearly shaken.

"I think your knee hit the table," I insisted. "Give us a few hours to get another cake, Katherine, and we'll shoot it again."

"It's Christine! And, you're driving me crazy! Cliff, this guy's driving me f--king crazy."

I guess we got the reaction CBS wanted, but could I turn her around? After all, unless things get really happy really fast when we do our reveal, the sequence is ruined.

"Smile, Christine. I'm Peter Funt. You're on 'Candid Camera.'"

After about half a second, which seemed to me like half an hour, she was smiling and laughing and declaring, "I wanted to murder you!"

Getting the first good take in the can is always the hardest part, so we cleaned up the mess and drove with renewed confidence to the studio where "Everybody Loves Raymond" was in production. The PR guy said we might want to pull the gag on Doris Roberts, who played Ray's mother on the show, as sort of a warm-up before doing Ray. I explained that we'd rather not press our luck, and he replied that Miss Roberts would arrive in five minutes.

I wondered how a 70-year-old actress, whose emphysema made it difficult to blow out the candle, and whose stature made it impossible for her to reach the top of the cake, could possibly add anything funny to our sequence. I called her "Daisy" a few times, the cake fell over, and we had another marvelous reaction.

Soon Ray Romano was at the door. Ray is a surprisingly shy person who off camera has more than his share of awkward moments. When I saw him a year later at the AT&T Pro-Am golf tournament in Pebble Beach, he was a nervous wreck. He and his pal Kevin James were on the driving range and they were sharing a set of clubs.

"What's with that?" I asked Kevin.

"Ray had a really bad feeling when he got here this morning," Kevin explained. "So he's having his clubs regripped again."

"Again?"

"He got new grips last week and it seemed to help."

Later, Ray told me, "If I hit more than 14 lousy shots today I'm dead."

"Why's that?"

"I've only prepared 14 funny excuses."

When Ray walked into our trailer on the Warner Bros. lot it was immediately clear that posing for a publicity picture with a big cake would be a struggle.

"You're the comedic portion of our publicity project," I said.

"That's a problem. That means I've got to be funny."

In our trial runs—and mercifully when Christine and Doris took their turns—the cake fell toward the camera and away from the performers. With Ray's luck, of course, the cake fell right on him.

"Smile, Ray! We're helping CBS celebrate its 50th birthday!"

"Is that its age or its demographic?" he shot back, quickly transforming himself from off-camera shy guy to on-camera genius.

And that should have brought us to the end of a perfect day, with a winning sequence. Instead, we had to drive to the set of "Cybill" and wait four hours so that I could have one of the worst professional experiences of my life.

Cybill Shepherd was doing her show before a live audience and CBS wasn't able to arrange our publicity photo until after the taping, at about 8:30. I stood in the wings and watched as Cybill and the other performers took their bows. After cameras were shut off her crew rolled out a table with a big cake. It seems Cybill's 48th birthday had been two days earlier, and this was to be a surprise celebration. Pumped by the enthusiastic audience, and apparently forgetting that she still had our photo shoot to worry about, Cybill decided to give everyone a good laugh. She plunged her head into the cake. As one assistant wiped frosting out of her nose, another reminded her that a still photographer was waiting in a trailer outside. That prompted the first in a night-long string of expletives. We waited for about an hour while Cybill retreated to her dressing room to shower, restyle her hair and redo her makeup.

"Let's do this in a hurry," Cybill said as she entered our trailer. "I'm tired, and I just stuck my damn face in a cake."

"What do you like to be called?" I asked.

"Cybill."

"Is that a Cher thing? Is there another name that goes with Cybill?"

"I can't do these pictures until you stop talking."

When I shoot a "Candid Camera" scene my mind is in overdrive. I'm editing the sequence in my head while figuring what to say next. Most important, I'm taking the subject's temperature, pushing as far as possible without crossing the line. If this had been our first take of the day I would have backed off, but based on our earlier success I plowed ahead.

"So it's Cybill, right?"

"The less you talk the better it will be for me," she snapped. "Don't crowd me!"

When we knocked over the cake the expression on Cybill's face was actually the best of the day. But viewers never got to see it.

"You're on 'Candid Camera,' Cybill. I'm Peter Funt."

"Is that what this was? I hate this so much, I can't tell you!"

I tried to block the door, thinking I could still redirect her emotions.

"That was grotesque. Get out of my way!"

She stormed across the parking lot, f-ing every step of the way, and began rounding up executives. Soon word filtered down from Cybill's dressing room that she was on the phone with her lawyer.

Cybill, just before the cake hit the fan.

CBS was thrilled with the scenes featuring Christine, Doris and Ray. The programming vice president phoned to tell me that we ought to do more of these catch-the-stars sequences. Then he said, "I was wondering if we should just go ahead and run the Cybill Shepherd piece whether she wants us to or not. Her series is about to be canceled anyway. What's she going to do, sue us?"

As I said, most network executives don't really understand what makes a good "Candid Camera" gag.

16 / PUPPET SHOW

THE CAT WAS OUT OF THE BAG. The rabbit was out of the hat. The genie was out of the bottle. The frosting was out of Cybill Shepherd's nose. And now there was no stopping CBS from sending me to catch VIPs.

Mike Naidus, the CBS publicist assigned to "Candid Camera," was worried about getting enough ink for a program that had, after all, been around for half a century. "If only we could prove to TV critics how thrilling it is to be caught," he said. (One thousand one, one thousand two, one thou...) "Could you catch TV critics?"

It wouldn't be easy. They're professional skeptics, presumably the hardest people to fool. And consider the downside: If we failed, they would have near-orgasmic pleasure writing about how Peter Funt couldn't trick them and that "Candid Camera" was a show whose time had passed. On the other hand, if we did pull it off, we'd have a major publicity coup.

TV writers were about to gather at the Ritz-Carlton in Pasadena for their semi-annual feeding frenzy with stars and network executives. What if the critics were given a room with no TV?

We scouted the hotel, and I obtained an outfit to play the bellman. We entrusted just one detail to CBS PR people; they would examine the booking list and let us know when each critic was due to check-in. [Note to self: Never leave production details to a network PR Department.] We arrived at the Ritz-Carlton to shoot the gag, only to find that all 80 writers had checked in the day before.

After much scurrying, the hotel staff turned up the fact that three writers had either missed their flights or were otherwise delayed and would be arriving a day late. Three. That wasn't much to work with—although at least they represented large markets: Detroit, Philadelphia and Denver. I don't know what we would have done if the latecomers had been from the Butte Beacon or the Oshkosh Observer.

The first writer to arrive was Mike Hughes of the *Detroit News*. I told him there had been some "water damage" in the far corner of his room, thus the strange looking plywood screen (hiding our camera). The only thing missing was the sign: NOTHING SUSPICIOUS HERE. But my father and I had used setups like this hundreds of times. We rely on the messy, unfinished look to throw people off. Imitators of "Candid Camera" probably would have spent thousands of dollars to rebuild the room with fake mirrors and sliding panels and fancy electronics. Their goal—misguided, I believe—would be to make the setup invisible to an unsuspecting subject. We, on the other hand, usually prefer to have our concealment screens very visible; only the camera is hidden. People see this thing, but they don't know what they're looking at.

"You don't understand," Hughes said, within seconds of learning there was no TV. "I'm a professional TV critic. I must have a television to do my work!"

Gail Shister of the *Philadelphia Inquirer* also became agitated about the missing TV, so we brought her a rusted portable with rabbit ears held on by duct tape. She ran to the phone. "This is Gail Shister from the *Philadelphia Inquirer.* This room is completely unacceptable! They just brought up a nine-inch TV that looks like it's held together with tape. And in the corner you've got something that looks like a puppet theater."

When she hung up I told her to smile, because the *puppet theater* was "Candid Camera." "You guys are sick," she exclaimed. "Thanks," I said. "I take that as a compliment."

A misconception about "Candid Camera" is that we're trying to target under-educated people, presumably because they are easier to fool. The actor Charles Grodin, who worked briefly on the "Candid Camera" staff in the 1960s, made this assertion in his autobiography, claiming that Dad liked to get "messengers and people like that; he didn't like to get professional people because they really get angry and they'll sue you." I mention Grodin's view in part because I was a big fan of his work. (If you haven't seen "The Heartbreak Kid," his bittersweet comedy about a guy who falls for another girl while on

his honeymoon, download it. The girlfriend is played by another of my favorites, Cybill Shepherd.) But I also cite Grodin's feelings because I believe he
misjudged "Candid Camera." While it is true that many of our scenes involve
temporary workers in office settings, gas station attendants, construction
workers and other regular folks, there was never a plan to single them out.
Most of the time, our subject is whoever walks through the door or comes
around the corner, regardless of their profession.

I was happy when we had the chance to take on real "professionals"—such
as a critic from Denver, who wrote the next day:

> By Joanne Ostrow
> Denver Post Television/Radio Critic
> PASADENA, Calif. – At the midseason TV critics' press tour,
> the fun starts even before you settle into your room. My mild-man-
> nered bellman, a white-haired gentleman with a youngish face, took
> me and a cart full of luggage to my room, explaining apologetically
> about recent water damage at the hotel.

I knew as soon as Ostrow and I walked into the room that she would
be a perfect subject . . .

> Now I was getting annoyed. My voice rising, I said I could not
> take this room because I was here as a TV critic and would have to
> watch certain closed-circuit screenings. I watch TV. It's what I do.
> My bellman offered to make a call. "Raoul, can you bring in
> a TV here?" Almost immediately a junior bellhop appeared with a
> dilapidated TV set smaller than my purse. "This one has been re-
> jected by another room but we can let you have it."
> I want a real TV, I said, nerves fraying.
> "Are you saying no? She's saying no, Raoul. Well, can you
> make it worth his while? You know what I mean? Say, $20 or some-
> thing?"
> Now I was furious. I need to call the desk, I said, moving to-
> ward the telephone.

I didn't allow her to call the desk. In real time the scene had gone on for several minutes and I thought we had plenty. I started to tell her it was "Candid Camera." She lunged at me and tried to remove my bellman's cap.

Smile! I laughed, I blushed, I felt like an imbecile.

I noticed the microphone clipped to his tie, I turned to look at the wooden barricaded structure that I now realized housed a camera. Now, of course, I recognized Funt, son of Allen, who created the show in 1948. I wondered how I must have looked, nose to the lens, while I examined the supposed "water damage." When you least expect it…

It was the only time I can ever recall being hugged by a TV critic.

Of all the strange things that go on here to generate ink – from glittery parties to logos fashioned out of chocolate – this was one of the wildest.

And, obviously, one of the most successful.

Successful, indeed, but we were in for one more pleasant surprise. The front desk called to say Fred Rogers from the award-winning PBS series "Mister Rogers' Neighborhood" happened to be checking in. Did we want to try the gag on him?

Of course! I escorted Rogers into the room and played my part just as I had for the critics. He was so friendly I fully expected him to plop down on the side of the bed and change into his sneakers. No matter what I said about the missing TV, he didn't seem to care. "Your room doesn't have a TV," I said for the third time as if to suggest no one could possibly get through the night without one.

What a perfect counterpoint to the remarks of the TV critics. "It's really okay," said Mister Rogers, trying to comfort me. "I have enough TV in my life as it is."

So sweet was this wonderful man that when I told him he was on "Candid Camera," he smiled . . . and then launched into a touching appeal to our viewers to donate to his sweater drive for the homeless.

A few days later I sent Mister Rogers and each critic a small medallion. It has a camera on one side and on the reverse an inscription:

You were caught in the act of being yourself
and were big enough to enjoy it.

17 / BLEEPIN' FUNNY

IN THE EARLIEST DAYS of "Candid Microphone" on radio in the mid-1940s, my father used a clever ruse to titillate listeners. A few times per show he'd edit out an innocent word or phrase and replace it with my mother's voice whispering, "Censored." Audiences always laughed at the thought that something dirty had been said, even though it hadn't. When "Candid Camera" came to television in 1948, Mom's voice was replaced by a bleep and a graphic that flashed "Censored!"

As my father and I learned during decades of eavesdropping, average people don't really curse much in routine conversation—even when mildly agitated—but audiences love to think otherwise.

Eventually network Standards and Practices people caught on to the fake bleeping and decreed there would be no censoring of clean words. I'm OK with that. But anyone who has worked in broadcast television or basic cable knows how messed up the standards are—starting with the fact that there really aren't any. TV is governed primarily by *fear*. Fear of government regulators, fear of advertisers, and fear of powerful religious groups. In sum: fear of anything that might affect profits.

This promotes a type of television that is suggestive, even gross at times, but not *dirty* according to most dictionaries. Drew Carey once developed a series for CBS called "WTF!" Winking furiously, the network insisted the title stood for "Wow That's Funny!"

The most powerful lobby in American television is the religious right. Conservative Christians are remarkably skilled at organizing letter-writing campaigns. They also arrange frighteningly effective advertiser boycotts.

Such viewers rarely complain about sexy scenes and titilating dialogue. They love double entendre, which prime-time broadcast television thrives upon. However, religious groups have a serious problem with dialogue that includes the words "God" or "Jesus." This presents a problem on "Candid Camera" because while our subjects curse less than you'd expect, they do frequently utter an exasperated "Oh, Jesus." For years CBS censors insisted I do something to correct this. I reminded them that if we bleeped "Jesus" we were inviting viewers to think something truly dirty had been said. They didn't care, because what mainstream broadcasters like best is the *perception* of naughtiness.

After much back and forth the network told me to have editors snip the end of "Jesus" so it became "geez."

♦ ♦ ♦

TV'S HYPOCRITICAL APPROACH TO CENSORSHIP was given its grandest showcase back in 1972, when George Carlin first took note of "Seven Words You Can Never Say on Television." Decades later his famous routine was recreated on stage at the Kennedy Center in a posthumous tribute to Carlin, but all the words were bleeped—not only for the PBS viewing audience but for the theatergoers as well. Many who saw the show believed the bleeped version played funnier than Carlin's original.

Most producers understand that when it comes to language, the sizzle has more appeal than the steak. Even on basic cable, the new generation of "reality" shows bleep like crazy, as do infotainment series like "The Daily Show," where curses are scripted so they can then be bleeped in a contrived bit of post-production.

Of the thousands of sequences I've shot for "Candid Camera," the one with the most bleeps-per-minute involved a change-making machine near an outdoor parking lot. The unit ordinarily gave four quarters for a dollar bill, but we rigged it so the machine dispensed 100 pennies. It was a quick, funny, self-working gag. In the editing room we realized that just about every patron—male and female—cursed at the pennies. Apparently folks are less careful with language when they're alone or, in this case, when they think they're alone.

Jimmy Kimmel has a segment on his late-night ABC program called "This Week in Unnecessary Censorship." He bleeps ordinary words in clips to make them seem obscene. How bleepin' dare he! That's my father's gimmick.

MANY PERFORMERS TRY to rescue a weak joke by punctuating it with a dirty word, much as writers use an exclamation point as a crutch! I'm no prude (especially after performing in numerous unfunny scenes with nude actresses for the ill-advised cable series in the mid-1980s known as "Playboy's Candid Camera"). But I find it disappointing that so many of today's comics lean on nasty language on pay-cable and streaming channels. The best worst example is John Oliver's brilliant HBO series, "Last Week Tonight." With biting comedy and eye-opening insight, Oliver manages to be funny while also educating his audience about important matters in current events. He cuts deeper than the topical stuff on "SNL's" Weekend Update or on "The Daily Show." But John Oliver uses more gratuitous profanity than anyone on television, a shame because his material is dynamite without it. Oliver's f-word cadence is so formulaic that it reminds me of a trick used by legendary baseball broadcaster Vin Scully. He kept a timer in the booth and whenever the sand ran through he'd give the score. Oliver seems to use a similar metric to insert four-letter words, whether they're needed or not.

STANDARDS AND PRACTICES DEPARTMENTS have always had more trouble with "Candid Camera" content than with material on scripted shows. Apparently the fact that something is *real* is unnerving to censors. A perfect example came when we shot a sequence in a parking lot outside a convenience store. When the subjects (unsuspecting people) returned to their cars they encountered an amorous young couple, kissing intensely and blocking the door. The bit was simple: How long would folks wait before saying something? And once they spoke, how would they handle it? One guy was mesmerized and, he told us later, didn't want to be rude to the lovers. So he just stood there. And stared. And stared some more.

A network vice president, whose name was not Bruce Flutz, became uncomfortable as he watched the footage. "Why stay with him so long?" he asked. I explained how a *build* works: The longer it lasts, the funnier it becomes. "Well," he said, "How do we know what's going on behind his dark glasses?"

That's a Hall of Fame entry in the annals of stupid network comments. Yes, the man was wearing sunglasses and . . . so what? I managed to let the remark go, but I refused to cut anything from the scene.

Those dark glasses must have hidden terrible thoughts.

In recent years network lawyers have become even tougher to deal with than censors. Something as innocuous as a logo on a subject's tee-shirt, which never used to be an issue, has become a legal Big Deal. That would never be an issue in a scripted sitcom or drama, since wardrobe is carefully planned. But with "Candid Camera" we don't pick the people or pay attention to what they're wearing. The lawyers usually ask us to blur the picture to obfuscate the logo. Aside from being unattractive this creates a distraction for viewers, so we try to push back as much as possible—but it's getting tougher to win such battles.

One annoying legal snafu came in 2014 when I was shooting a scene outside a gas station. We attached the restroom key to ludicrously large objects, such as the wheel of a car, "for your convenience, so we don't lose the key." This particular gas station had an old Coca-Cola sign painted on an outside wall—a vintage ad, more than 30 years old. Viacom's lawyer wouldn't allow it to be shown in the background. We finally had to contact Coca-Cola for written permission—which was provided once the Coke heads stopped laughing about the foolishness of our request.

But there's more to the story, underscoring the fickle nature of television's rules. We allowed a crew from "Good Morning America" to tag along so we could do a secondary gag: For one take, Linda Gulley pretended to be the unsuspecting Candid subject. When ABC's reporter joined me for the "happy reveal," Linda feigned anger and threw her soda in my face. We successfully caught ABC's shocked reporter, and then did the real reveal with her. Funny thing: ABC didn't care about the Coke sign at all.

JOHNNY CARSON ONCE ADVISED, "Never use a big word when a little filthy one will do." The trouble for some folks is that certain big words sound "dirty" even though they are perfectly clean.

We hired temporary clerks to work at a greeting card company. "Our problem," I explained, "is that the writers occasionally use profanity, and we can't risk having smut in our cards." So I gave the clerks a list of words, and asked that they separate them into a CLEAN column and a DIRTY column.

The words:

Seersucker • Titillate

Torque • Matriculate

Fugue • Thespian

One man told me that "thespian" was definitely dirty, though he wasn't certain what it meant. "It's a word I read in a book," he said, "but I can't remember how it was used."

"Oh," I said. "Was it a clean book or a dirty book?"

One woman concluded that thespian was the only clean word. Each of the other words, she explained, had a very "bad sound."

Censorship, no matter who's doing it, remains one of the most entertaining things on television.

18 / TRIALS AND TREPIDATIONS

IT WAS A STEAMY JUNE DAY in Arizona, and for me and "Candid Camera" things were about to get hotter.

We had tried for weeks to find a location that would allow us to do a gag poking fun at airport security. This was 2001, a few months before 9/11, and "security" was far different than it is today—it was laid-back and even risible. We finally found an amenable airport in Bullhead City, which serves the nearby gambling community of Laughlin, Nevada. I would pose as an officer, claiming the metal detector wasn't working and instructing passengers to lie down on the conveyor belt and ride through the X-ray machine.

We built a phony machine—a large empty box with holes cut in each end, placed over a rented conveyor belt. We attached a few lights to the outside of the box, along with our version of the classic sign: EVERYTHING SAID WILL BE TAKEN SERIOUSLY. It's important to stress that there were no actual X-rays involved; in fact, the real X-ray machine was several hundred feet away. Airport management reviewed the gag with the Federal Aviation Administration and obtained clearance. The night before our taping we tested our prop, with the airport's security chief riding back and forth several times on her stomach, laughing all the way. The next morning we double-checked everything and then randomly selected our first subject: Philip Zelnick, 35, from Southern California, who later gave his occupation as "unemployed fitness trainer."

Zelnick laughed when I told him he'd have to go through the X-ray machine, then asked, "Where's the Candid Camera?" Had that happened later in the day I probably would have stopped, but often we allow the first take to continue even if it doesn't seem worthy of a spot in the finished show, to allow the crew to evaluate audio and video and for me to work on my patter. Zelnick

rolled back and forth twice and then, as he was getting off the conveyor, his sweat pants caught between the belt and its metal frame, pinching his thigh. He yelled "ouch."

After using the manager's private restroom, he showed us a small bruise on his thigh. I asked if he wanted a Band-Aid or medical attention and he declined and left to catch his flight to California. Meanwhile, our crew rechecked the conveyor and after concluding that the mishap was a fluke, we continued the day's shooting without incident.

I phoned Zelnick the next day and offered to pay any medical bills he might have, but he said there were none. A few days later we received a letter from a Beverly Hills attorney who stated that Zelnick was now his client. We turned the matter over to our insurance company and for the next two years things got progressively distorted and expensive. To begin with, when 9/11 happened the world's view about airport security changed in a nightmarish flash. Zelnick fired his lawyer and found one who believed 9/11 upped the stakes enough for a high-profile lawsuit.

Until you've been sued—in a court higher than small claims—you never really understand the incredible obstacles in the system we value so much, not to mention the time and money required to simply defend oneself. Just to get a court date in Los Angeles takes over a year. Zelnick's lawyer subpoenaed just about every piece of paper and computer file we had generated in the previous two years, plus the unedited videotape. He also took depositions from numerous employees of both "Candid Camera" and the airport administration. Had we cut off Zelnick's leg rather than bruised it, the legal process wouldn't have been much different.

About six months prior to trial, Zelnick and his lawyer shifted their tactics from a straightforward legal case to a strategy that more resembled a PR campaign. Zelnick began showing up on TV talk programs with the un-aired tape we provided under subpoena. Incredibly, six pictures from the tape were printed in a spread in *People* magazine, under the headline "Reality Bites." Of course the tape and photos showed very little about any injury to Zelnick; indeed, the video actually supported our contention that the mishap, while regrettable, was not serious. But the sheer volume of coverage gave the impression that something significant had occurred. Then Zelnick turned up on NBC's "Dateline," describing his experience as a "train wreck." He claimed that during the four-minute sequence, "I could hear people in the airport, other passengers, laughing at me, speculating that I could be a criminal."

The reports by *People* and "Dateline" were inspired—as are so many stories in U.S. media—by coverage in *The New York Times*. This error-filled account was especially painful for me because I spent years writing for *The Times* and admiring its standards. When reporter Adam Liptak phoned me to say that he was writing about the legal problems facing reality shows I was eager to speak, assuming *The Times* would set the record straight. The story that Liptak wrote could be used in journalism classes as an example of careless reporting as well as the peripheral damage that can be caused when a powerful media voice like *The Times* gets a story wrong and is unwilling to correct it.

In describing Zelnick's experience, Liptak wrote: "A security guard made him lie down on a conveyor belt and pass through the X-ray machine.

It left him, he said, humiliated and 'bleeding all over the place.'" Liptak apparently never saw the tape. There was never so much as a molecule of blood—as confirmed later in the trial. And *The Times* account never explained that the "X-ray machine" was only a prop, leaving readers to assume it was a real X-ray unit. Later in the story there were no quotes and no attribution when Liptak wrote: "Mr. Funt did not let Mr. Zelnick in on the joke until he emerged bruised, bloody and screaming in pain." This sentence is about as irresponsible as journalism can get. Zelnick didn't "emerge" from anything, he got off of the conveyor; while he did have a single bruise, there was no bloodshed whatsoever, and he certainly wasn't screaming. Liptak's only possible sources for this account would have been Philip Zelnick or his representatives—people seeking to profit from a lawsuit regarding the incident.

Additionally damning was that *The Times* story, although centering on Zelnick, lumped our case together with other "reality TV" litigation, including a suit by a woman who "said she suffered severe pain and lasting injury after being hung for 40 minutes with her back bent unnaturally in a harness" as part of a CBS pilot entitled "Culture Shock," and a couple who sued MTV after checking into the Hard Rock Hotel in Las Vegas and finding a corpse in the bathtub, arranged by a program called "Harassment."

OUR TRIAL WAS HELD in Superior Court in Los Angeles before Judge Mel Red Recana, with TV coverage provided by HBO and CourtTV. Everyone, from judge to lawyers to jurors, gets *big-deal-itis* when television is present—after all, if this weren't a big deal, why would TV be there? And when jurors are asked to determine damages, how are they going to vote for a meager sum in a televised trial? That's like being taken to a fancy restaurant and feeling foolish ordering just a burger.

In his opening statement Zelnick's lawyer Andrew Jones said: "The evidence will show that Peter Funt, Candid Camera, and the Mojave Airport District violated and trampled on Phil's rights: his right to self-respect, his right not to be humiliated or embarrassed in public; that he was held up to public ridicule in the name of reality TV. It will show that they fooled Phil and made him appear a fool in public to the laughter of bystanders. ... Now, you have to understand, the plaintiff has no objection to a show, a humorous show, that innocently captures some amusing moment in life. You know, a person coughs and his false teeth fall out, and the bystanding crowd is aghast."

(I have to interrupt here to applaud Andy's comedic touch. The old "false teeth bit" always gets big laughs.)

"This is not reality TV. There's nothing real about this. It was contrived. It was a charade, a charade of lies. ... The evidence will show that there's a need for punitive damages to make the defendants an example, to prevent them from doing this again, and to send a message to the reality TV—humiliation TV—genre that it is not okay to step over the line."

And with that, Zelnick's case was apparent. It wasn't about the bruise on his leg; in fact it wasn't about him at all. The jury was being asked to punish "reality TV." Of course producers of the truly vile reality shows couldn't have cared less. They believe lawsuits are part of doing business. But, they always settle out of court; only a prideful idiot like Peter Funt would allow this type of thing to reach a jury—on CourtTV, no less.

The opening statement by my lawyer, Robert Baker, was straightforward, bordering on boring. Although the judge had ruled it inadmissible, Rob tried to sneak in the fact that "Candid Camera" had never been taken to court, nor had any of our subjects ever been injured. He also emphasized that while Zelnick was suing over alleged "humiliation" suffered during our sequence, it was *he* who distributed the tape of his scene for broadcast on "Dateline" and other programs.

After opening arguments, Andrew Jones called me to the stand and showed the jury the unedited tape of Zelnick's encounter with me at the airport. In an odd attempt to make me look foolish, Jones asked if I'd be willing to lie down on a table in the courtroom, to simulate the act of riding the airport conveyor. I think he was surprised when I bounced out of the witness chair and gave it a try, although to the jury and TV viewers I probably looked pretty strange flopping around on my stomach on the attorney's table.

When I returned to the stand, I said, "I assumed you were going to say,

'Smile. You're on CourtTV.'"

Then came an exchange that was undoubtedly a turning point in the trial. I knew it was coming, and I knew I was about to allow my pride and principles to get in the way of winning a court case.

AJ: So what's your feeling now about putting on a uniform and a badge? Is it appropriate to take an unsuspecting citizen off the street and force them to do something under the color of law? Are you going to continue to do that?

PF: I wouldn't ever use the word "force." But I certainly wouldn't hesitate to play that part or a similar part for a similar sequence if we had it on our agenda next week.

AJ: Okay.

Jones had what he wanted. My answer made clear that I hadn't "learned my lesson" about playing the part of a security guard—the "offense" which Jones seemed to think required the most severe punitive damages.

Next it was Zelnick's turn on the witness stand, and most of what he said was predictable, except for his claim that at the airport he had a ballpoint pen in his pocket which caused a puncture wound in his other leg—an injury he never mentioned to anyone at the airport.

Jones' partner Nicholas Wagner delivered his closing argument:

"If you or I impersonated a police officer for profit, you know where we would go? We would go to jail. You know where Mr. Funt goes? He goes to the bank. ... The basis of Mr. Funt's business is to exploit enough people, infringe upon their privacy and their personal freedoms and liberties to do what they want to do. ... This case is obviously bigger than Mr. Zelnick, and hence, all the media attention. As you've probably figured out, it's pretty much a case of first impression. A case like this hasn't been brought before and it's against the number one reality show and it's obviously a big deal because what happens in this courtroom can change the course of this type of reality show."

The specific charges, when reduced to legal terms on the jury forms, were: "negligence, battery, intentional misrepresentation, intentional inflic-

My legal training consisted of this "Candid Camera" gag in Denver.

tion of emotional distress, and false imprisonment." It's interesting to note that in civil trials the standard for judgment is less than in criminal cases where there must be proof "beyond a reasonable doubt." The civil standard, as the jury was instructed, requires only "a preponderance of the evidence"— meaning, "evidence that has more convincing force than that opposed to it."

Even more vexing than the evidentiary standards were the unique circumstances of the case itself, prompting one juror to ask the judge about the charges. "A lot of these questions seem straightforward," he said, " but then again they don't. I guess what I'm asking is: Should we answer them ignoring the concept of a joke? Or should we answer them acknowledging the context of a joke?" The judge didn't have an answer.

THE JURY DELIBERATED for about three hours, then found "Candid Camera" and me liable for negligence, false imprisonment and intentional misrepresentation, but cleared us on the claims of battery and intentional infliction of emotional distress. They awarded Zelnick $2,100 in compensatory damages from us, plus $400 from the airport. It would have been nice, at least in my view, if things had ended right there. But the findings of "false imprisonment" and "intentional misrepresentation" created the need for phase two: a mini-trial to determine what punitive damages, if any, should be awarded. As phase two began, the lawyers uncovered the fact that the jury foreman had written some dollar amounts in the upper right corner of the court's form: *"Candid Camera $400,000. Peter Funt $200,000."* Apparently the jurors had already considered punitive damages—something they were instructed not to do—before hearing arguments relating to that portion of the trial. Robert Baker demanded a mistrial. Judge Recana refused, but instructed the jury to ignore their own conclusions until after the arguments were completed.

During a recess I asked Rob, "What if I acted as my own lawyer for this phase?" and began to tell him about a "Candid Camera" sequence a few years earlier at a real courthouse in Denver where I played the prosecuting attorney. I grilled witnesses with fist-pounding theatrics—using elaborate charts of the "crime scene" and evidence of "DNA taken from a dress."

"I'd love to see a copy of that," said Rob, "it sounds funny." He was straining to be polite, since we both knew that playing a lawyer on TV doesn't qualify anyone to attempt it in real life. Even so, we headed back to the courtroom, with me as attorney:

PF: Well, hello. This is either my big opportunity to do well on my own behalf, or my final opportunity to make a fool of myself. ... I don't think I need to tell you I'm no lawyer and I never went to law school. In fact, until this trial I had never set foot in a courtroom in my life except on one occasion, and that's when I —

NW: Objection, your honor. Outside the evidence.

JUDGE: Overruled. Go ahead.

PF: When I played the part of a lawyer in one of our "Candid Camera" sequences. But this is my first time in a courtroom, and certainly the first time in my life I've ever been sued, the first time my company,

Candid Camera, has ever been sued.

NW: Objection. Outside the evidence.

JUDGE: Sustained. Please disregard, ladies and gentlemen.

PF: You're going to be asked now whether you want to award punitive damages in this case. You've already awarded Mr. Zelnick some damages in phase one, and that would be in addition to any settlements that have been arrived at in this case.

NW: Objection, your honor.

JUDGE: Overruled. Go ahead, please.

PF: I imagine that when I'm finished speaking, one of the other lawyers will tell you argumentatively that this is some kind of grandstand play: don't pay too much attention to him because he does this for a living; this is what he did in this case; he sweet talks people; he, you know, sells people a bill of goods. Well, that may be what I do for a living, but it's not my reason for speaking to you now. And I dare say, that's what a good lawyer does for a living anyway. ... I went to the people in charge of security at the airport and said, "You're in charge of security. Is it okay with you if I wear a uniform and impersonate one of you guys?" And they said, "sure." What was I supposed to do? Argue with them?"

AJ: Make no mistake. Mr. Funt is an actor! He's a showman! He's making a personal appeal to you, and he's doing so for your sympathy. ... I think you have to recognize there is a message to be sent. This is the grandfather of reality TV. There has to be a message that there are limits and boundaries.

THE JURY DECIDED we should pay Zelnick $300,000 in punitive damages. It was far less than the $600,000 the jurors had envisioned earlier, so I imagine my effort to represent myself paid off. In the end, the jurors couldn't really separate this pre-9/11 event from their own post-9/11 mindsets; they couldn't make a distinction between actual "false imprisonment" and the "Candid

Camera" kind; they didn't seem to focus on the fact that if I was allowed by the authorities to step in as an officer, then I wasn't "impersonating" one, I *was* one. But, apparently, they did accept the notion that this was a legitimate way to put producers of other "reality" shows on notice.

We immediately appealed. Several landmark decisions by the U.S. Supreme Court have served to limit the size of punitive damage awards by requiring that they be more closely tied, mathematically, to compensatory damages. The Supreme Court guideline called for a "single digit multiplier" in most cases. Thus, if Zelnick was awarded $2,100 from us as compensatory damages, the ceiling on punitive damages would be nine times that amount, or $18,900. There are exceptions, but our case never impressed most outside observers as exceptional.

Zelnick's lawyers quickly settled with our attorneys before the case reached the appeals court. (As part of that settlement I am prohibited from disclosing its terms.)

For all the talk during the trial about "sending a message," it turns out the only people getting the message loud and clear were those at Fireman's Fund. Within hours they canceled our insurance.

19 / RENT-A-WRECK

DURING MY FINAL YEAR OF HIGH SCHOOL I played the part of a woman in the senior-class play. This could have been an awful repeat of my experience at Camp Lenox ten years earlier when I was coerced into the role of Buttercup, but fortunately I was cast as a macho writer for the *Daily Star* newspaper, Bill Hastings, who takes over the advice column "Aunt Phoebe." To maintain the column's popularity, he must make readers believe he's a woman.

I loved the exhilaration of being in a theater, under bright lights, hoping to persuade an audience that the price of a ticket was money well spent.

It doesn't work that way in television. A "stage," for example, isn't a stage at all; it's a flat, hangar-size building in which sets are constructed, with camera equipment and lights rolled into place. The audience, if there is one, is seated around the set in temporary bleachers. Moreover, audience members don't buy tickets, they are frequently paid to attend. This works well for production companies because with many boring breaks between scenes and frequent retakes, it's best if audience members are as professional at their jobs as performers and crew are at theirs. If audience reactions aren't what's hoped for—especially after the same scene is shot several times—laughs are added in post-production, in a fraud known as "sweetening."

No wonder many television performers yearn for a chance to work in a legitimate theater, before a properly paying audience.

IN THE SUMMER OF 2015, with the TV Land experience behind me, I put together a theater version of "Candid Camera," combining our best video clips with live comedy. For the first show, Brian Courrejou and I packed the necessary props and drove down California's Highway 101 to the Clark Center for the Performing Arts in Arroyo Grande. Neither of us had ever been inside this 617-seat theater; in fact we hadn't been to Arroyo Grande, a scruffy city of roughly 18,000 people, some 150 miles north of Los Angeles. I had paid $2,750 to rent the theater on a Saturday night, in what seemed like a clever way to finally perform on a real stage and make some easy money. Oy.

The first whiff of trouble came in mid-afternoon when the stage manager unlocked the place. The smell was fresh paint. "We do maintenance and refurbishing during July and August," he explained, "because there are no shows." The Clark Center's schedule ran from September to May, and now it was July 11. Most residents and tourists were at beaches, a few miles west. How had I managed to overlook such critical details before laying out money for a theater? I'm not quite sure, except that I naively assumed that if we built it (a show), they would come (an audience).

At 8:01 p.m. I walked on stage to the enthusiastic applause of about 200 people. Fortunately, when you look into powerful theatrical spotlights you can't really see the people—or the unoccupied seats. I began:

"A quick announcement before we get started. During tonight's performance, the taking of photographs is expressly *permitted*. (Laughs) Look, I've spent most of my career taking your picture without permission, so I can't very well stand in your way now." (Appreciative chuckle)

I mocked the city:

"Fascinating place, Arroyo Grande...named after a steep gully and a 16-ounce coffee." (Big laugh)

The adrenaline rush on stage is unique. Getting laughs from an appreciative audience is exhilarating. And taking a show on the road, even a dusty stretch of Highway 101, is magical.

When the accounting was complete, I had lost about $50 on the big Arroyo Grande show, which I declared a success.

I began renting more theaters across California: The Rio in Santa Cruz...the Poway Center for Performing Arts near San Diego...the Indian Wells Theatre in Palm Desert. Each deal had its quirks. The Rio, a beautiful old place built in 1946 to house one of the first 3-D Cyclorama movie screens, has a dressing room on the second floor above the lobby. The only way to reach the stage is to make your entrance by walking down the aisle. In San Diego, we arranged for the *Union-Tribune* newspaper to pay half our costs and run free ads in return for a pre-show meet-and-greet with subscribers. Only later did we discover that the paper had selected a theater in the suburb of Poway because, as a representative explained, "That's our weakest area where we have the fewest readers." In Indian Wells, the manager conceded, "I was surprised you picked us. Our theater is normally used for college events, and the college is closed for vacation."

Not one to give up easily, I rented theaters across Oregon, Arizona and Colorado. Driving to the Magnolia Theater in Fort Collins, Colorado (elevation 5,100 feet) I developed a bad nose bleed, which persisted throughout the entire show. For two hours I held the microphone with one hand and a Kleenex pressed against my nose with the other. The audience was certain it was a gag and some people were clearly annoyed when the joke turned out to be: There's no joke.

Moving to the East Coast, I rented theaters in Tarrytown, New York; Great Barrington, Massachusetts; and Ridgefield, Connecticut—with my son, Danny, and niece Katie joining the cast. The show was getting better at each stop, but I wasn't making any money. By renting theaters my company was forced to function as a promoter, sending press releases, running newspaper and radio ads, and sometimes even handling ticket sales. Arranging these things from across the country was difficult, especially when theater owners refused to share mailing lists or include our show in their promotions.

The Ridgefield show drew a disappointing crowd on a night when, unbeknownst to us, the Winter Christmas Carnival was being held a few blocks away.

I asked the theater manager if she knew of any experts—agents, promoters, marketing people—who might have some advice. "I know of a man who is really good at stage shows," she said. "Unfortunately, he's across the country, quite far away."

"Where's that?" I asked.

"Somewhere in California," she explained, and went on to describe the town about three miles from my house.

Two weeks later, Brian Swanson listened patiently as I recounted my frustrations with theater rentals. I said I'd like to continue, but only if I could quit losing money. He sipped his coffee and said, as politely as possible, "You've got this whole thing backwards. You shouldn't be paying theaters, they should be paying you."

It was as if a doctor had just told me my foot wouldn't hurt so much if I took the nail out of my shoe.

We've since done dozens of stage shows at venues all across the country, never again losing money. Our "LOL Tour," as we began calling it, is a niche show that only occasionally sells out, but pleases audiences of all ages.

IF YOU DO ENOUGH SHOWS you become quite a conoisseur of "green rooms" and dressing rooms. Some are remarkably lavish; others look like they haven't been cleaned since the last ten rock bands came through. We provide a "tech rider," listing our show requirements. I like to keep the catering part simple: fresh fruit, chips, coffee with nonfat milk, tea, Diet Coke and bottled water. That's about it. Some artists, however, make outlandish demands, the most legendary of which was contained in the rider used by Van Halen: "M&Ms. Warning: Absolutely no brown ones." Picky as it seemed, there was method to this madness. As David Lee Roth explained in a 2012 interview about the band's complicated on-stage set-up: "If I came backstage, having been one of the architects of this lighting and staging design, and I saw brown M&Ms on the catering table, then I guarantee the promoter had not read the contract rider, and we would have to do a serious line check."

Danny and I favor a rigid routine on show days, pre-game as we call it, with every move calculated. A stage routine is like a golfer's routine. I used to have a golf coach at Pebble Beach named Laird Small (when you take lessons, your teacher is an "instructor"; after you've paid more than the price of a luxury car, you're entitled to refer to that person as a "coach"). Laird knows a great deal about correcting a hook or a slice, but he's also an expert on the mental part of sports. He noticed that as I walked up the fairway I stared at the ground, probably dwelling on my last mistake. "Look at the tops of the trees," he advised.

There are so many good reasons to do that: (1) it forces better posture as you walk, (2) your breathing is more relaxed, and (3) your focus shifts to the task ahead, not the errors to be left behind. Danny and I have adopted that as our credo for going forward in our careers: Look at the tops of the trees.

After our shows I rush to the theater lobby to shake hands and pose for photos. Some performers charge money for this as part of "VIP ticket packages," but I do it happily for free because of something I learned from the talk-show host Phil Donahue years earlier. One of my first assignments for *The New York Times* was to cover a taping of Donahue's show during his visit to Manhattan. The program was at the height of its popularity and the taping was at Madison Square Garden's Felt Forum, with 4,300 people attending. I wrote:

> For most of "Donahue's" audience, the highlight of the day comes after the taping. The producer had announced that "Phil will stand out front and say goodbye until every last person has left this building." So with jacket off and sleeves rolled up, he stood in the Garden lobby like a minister awaiting comments from his parishioners. ... He shook each hand and received several thousand pecks on the cheek.

Later I asked Phil Donahue why he bothered. "I'm grateful," he said. It was as simple as that.

MY FIRST VISIT TO A REAL THEATER came at age ten, when my aunt Dorothy took me to "The Music Man" at the Majestic on West 44th Street. Is there anything more magical in the entertainment spectrum than a live stage show? Can there be any more indelible memory than one's first glimpse of Broadway? I still know all the words, including the complicated lyrics to "Ya Got Trouble." Robert Preston's performance as Prof. Harold Hill filled me with hope. He was a leading man without the usual good looks, a dancer who couldn't really dance, a singer who was average at best and *spoke* his way through most songs.

In late February, 2020, over 550 people attended our show in Morristown, New Jersey—a terrific turnout by our modest standards.

We had no way of knowing the lights were about to go out.

20 / GIMME SHELTER

BACK IN 2014 I set up a gag at a restaurant in Carmel for which everyone in the room—including my wife, Amy, seated in the corner—was working for "Candid Camera." Everyone, that is, except occupants of one table in the center. As the unsuspecting patrons got settled and examined the menu they noticed that the waitress, busboy and all other diners were wearing surgical masks. Yes, blue surgical masks, the very type that would become ubiquitous in our lives six years later. The gag was great. The discussions, captured by a microphone hidden on the table, were funny. We simply had no idea how prescient it was.

In 2020, soon after I returned from the stage show in Morristown, the pandemic forced a halt to TV production and wiped out the slate of shows we had booked for the next 18 months.

Sheltering became a way of life for all of us—with contact-free meals, daily deliveries from Amazon and plenty of Zooming. Early on I did a remote interview for British television. The producers were eager to dumb-down the process for me so they FedEx'd a small camera, lavalier microphone, circle light and collapsible green screen. Have you unwrapped a green screen? Be careful! The metal frame snapped open explosively, leaving a bloody gash across the bridge of my nose. (Philip Zelnick probably would have sued the British bastards.)

Have you ever tried to refold a green screen? I phoned a friend in TV production for advice and learned that it's practically impossible; however, there are dozens of YouTube tutorials on this topic. In one, a guy named "Lo Knows" informs viewers, "It's a convoluted mess of twisting, folding and more twisting."

With the world collapsing around us, Trump went on TV each afternoon saying, "Relax. Inject bleach. It will all pass." Meanwhile, toilet paper was sold out all over town. When I checked Amazon I was surprised to find that it, too, was, uh, wiped out—except for one offer of four rolls for $72. Meanwhile, late-night radio carried ads for a month's supply of freeze-dried food and for gold coins to use when the banks fail. I seriously considered ordering a hand-cranked radio, "essential if the power grid goes down."

MANY OF US OVERDOSED ON YOUTUBE during coronavirus confinement. I noticed that videos are tracked: watching one leads to countless suggestions for others. One morning I heard a TV commentator mention Manhattan's deserted streets, so I searched for that and, sure enough, YouTube delivered a live shot from Times Square. When I refreshed YouTube its algorithm had apparently determined that I'm a fan of random street views, so it suggested one in Jackson Hole, Wyoming, overlooking the Pizzeria Caldera in Town Square. Another click and I was transported to an intersection in La Grange, Kentucky.

The Kentucky view included train tracks. Naturally, YouTube assumed I'd enjoy a live stream of rail yards in La Plata, Missouri, with a description boasting, "Amtrak's Southwest Chief passenger train stops here twice a day!"

YouTube then determined that I must also love subways. This resulted in "Good Samaritans Confront Man with Hatchet on NYC Subway Train," which led to "The Ugliest NYC Subway Station," and then to "New York's Incredible Subway Dancers."

After a while YouTube must have concluded: This guy is really into transportation! So I watched a fly-over video of a place in Victorville, California, where some 400 commercial planes were parked during the coronavirus shutdown. And that took me to "10 Things You Should Not Say to Car Dealers." Eager to escape the transportation thread, I tried to trick the computer by searching for "suggested YouTube videos." The first recommendation—and I'm not making this up—was a video titled "YouTube Suggested Videos Suck!"

Clearly, YouTube knows itself even better than it knows me.

♦ ♦ ♦

AMONG THE MODEST PLEASURES OF SHELTERING at home were daily deliveries from Amazon—for instance, two "Value Size" packages of Kellogg's Special K with a "touch of cinnamon" or the bottle of Shout Advanced Ultra Concentrated Gel Set-In Stain Brush Laundry Stain Remover.

Some delivery people wore surgical masks and latex gloves. About those gloves: If worn for several hours aren't they covered with even more germs than bare hands?

At the start of the pandemic I was eager to stock up on personal protective equipment—what commentators and candidates called "PPE"—so I scoured Amazon's site for hand sanitizer and wound up ordering the only thing in stock, a product called Beauty New. It arrived a week later—by China Post, direct from Shenzhen, about 680 miles from Wuhan. You can't make this stuff up. (Actually, you can. But that wouldn't be any fun.)

♦ ♦ ♦

DURING SHELTERING I found myself doing more things online, and that led to the recurrent problem of forgotten passwords. Most days I couldn't gain access without clicking "Forgot Password" to begin the damnable process of getting a new one.

Trouble is, I can't remember answers to the Security Questions. What was the first street you lived on? Apparently when I set-up the account I typed "Mt. Airy Road," but this time I entered "Mount Airy Road." Sorry: Your answer does not match our records for this account.

Who was your favorite school teacher? Sheesh. Did I give them Mr. Brooks the tennis coach who made me captain so I wouldn't switch to baseball? Or was it Miss Fox, the fifth grade teacher on whom I had such a crush that I phoned her at home every night and chatted for over an hour?

What is your favorite breakfast cereal? Do they mean before age ten, when I ate only Kellogg's Sugar Corn Pops? Or later in life when someone convinced me that Special K is healthy? Or are they talking about hotel breakfast buffets where Fruit Loops are free?

Many of the sites I try to access tell me, "Your User ID and/or Password are incorrect." Come on! Which? I have five or six IDs and maybe two dozen passwords. Do you have any idea how many possible combinations that is? Well, I don't either—but it's too many to try before being notified that "For your protection, your account has been locked."

I tried using one simple password, even if it didn't have the *strength* that most sites recommend. Here's the problem with that: If your password is, say, StephCurry, but you forgot that you entered Curry with a capital C, then it won't work. And when you reset that password you'll probably be told that it's "Too similar to a recently used password."

So, you make it StephCurry#. I'm warning you: forget that last part and you'll wind up changing it to StephCurry@ and then StephCurry+ and pretty soon you're back with a Security Question that you can't answer.

I often stare at the screen counting the little dots in my "hidden" password, hoping for a clue. Ten dots suggests it might be StephCurry; 11 dots might mean StephCurry#.

I have watched several YouTube videos on how to set-up a "Single Password" for all accounts. Let's just say I did worse with those tutorials than I did in high school French class.

Meanwhile, I got a new credit card through American Airlines. The last thing I needed during the pandemic was another credit card, but this was one of those deals offering 40,000 free miles. When I tried to log in to pay my first bill I was notified that my User ID was incorrect. I entered my gmail address, which usually works, but not this time. In desperation I tried StephCurry and LeBronJames#, but no luck. I finally got a question right—having to do with a "favorite pet"—and was notified that I would be emailed a link with which I could "retrieve" my User ID.

After several clicks CitiBank informed me: "Your User ID is Peter Funt." Now, how could I have ever guessed that?

♦ ♦ ♦

I LOVE SPORTS, but the pandemic-style games were beyond bizarre with piped in crowd noise and cardboard fans. Major League Baseball came up with special rules: No showering at the ballpark. No sunflower seeds. No high-fives. And my personal favorite: No spitting.

A lot of baseball's rich history of spitting during games stems from players' passion for chewing tobacco. But ballplayers also have the nasty habit of spitting on their hands before swinging a bat—as if batting gloves, pine tar and rosin aren't enough to provide a good grip. Fielders spit into their mitts between pitches—as if oils and creams won't keep the pocket supple.

Many players simply spit to make a point. Dr. Mary Lamia, writing in *Psychology Today,* sought to make sense of what she called "the deliberate and unconstrained" act of spitting in baseball. "If spitting can protect a person by evoking disgust in the observer," she reasoned, "then, given the consequences, it might be considered as an aggressive or contemptuous display... Evoking disgust in another person can be a way to cope with, or disguise, one's own anxiety."

Oddly, while ballplayers were forbidden from spitting during games during the pandemic, they were required to spit before games. MLB avoided nasal swabs by using a virus test for which players spit into a tube.

And what about the most famous aspect of the game's fondness for saliva, the spitball? Loading up the baseball with "foreign substances" was outlawed by Major League Baseball before the 1920 season. That didn't stop pitchers from doctoring the baseball—it simply compelled them to be more clever about it. In his 1974 autobiography "Me and the Spitter," Gaylord Perry detailed how he applied Vaseline to his zipper before dabbing some on the ball—because umpires were disinclined to inspect a player's crotch area too closely. Naturally, MLB addressed the dilemma pitchers faced. Section 5.1 of the new pandemic protocol stated: "All pitchers may carry a small wet rag in their back pocket to be used for moisture in lieu of licking their fingers."

Record books will need an asterisk for pitchers who overachieved in 2020 with the baffling ragball.

◆ ◆ ◆

EVEN A ROUTINE MEDICAL EXAM was an adventure during the pandemic. My cardiologist's nurse phoned to explain that due to the coronavirus my checkup would be conducted *telephonically*. I assumed she was referring to "telehealth," which had been in the news a lot.

"How will this work?" I asked. "Will we use Zoom?"

"Oh, the doctor doesn't do video exams," she replied.

"Well, then..."

"He'll call you Tuesday at 1:30."

"On the phone?"

"Yes."

A few days before my appointment I received the standard reminder that if I had to cancel I should do so at least 24 hours in advance to avoid "penalty charges."

As the exam call began I made a strategic error by asking, "How have you been?"

The kindly doc, who has treated me for several years, explained that during the pandemic he has not been swimming at his club and is exercising on a treadmill in his garage. "I worked my way up to six miles at a steady jog," he said. "But I think I pushed it too much. I wrenched something in my back and it hurts to just tie my running shoes."

"That's awful," I said. "A few years ago I found a good physical therapist who specializes in sports medicine. I could email you his number."

"Please do. I've been having a difficult time emotionally during the pandemic. They have us wearing these spacesuits during surgeries at the hospital, and it's claustrophobic."

"Have you tried listening to music with earbuds?" I asked. "I read that music helps to soothe people who work in confined spaces."

"I just haven't been myself. My wife is away and I'm home alone."

"Many local restaurants use Grubhub or other services to bring food right to your door. You know that, right?"

"I'll try it. But what about you, Peter. How are you feeling?"

"Fine."

"Are you still taking the same meds?"

"Yes."

"OK, then let's schedule another check-up in six months."

A few days later the bill arrived: $238.

Seeing the charge seemed to make my blood pressure spike. I considered phoning the doctor about it, but I wasn't sure how much more telehealth my insurance would cover.

♦ ♦ ♦

AS THE JOKE HAD IT, nine months from the start of the pandemic—right around January 2021—the nation experienced a baby boom. After all, some activities are better suited to sheltered lifestyles than others.

In addition to making babies, there was a crush of pandemic garden propagation. Enforced free time in spring led to a summer season with some of the saddest little fruits and vegetables ever seen on kitchen tables. Many of us began gardening furiously in April—some folks for the first time in their lives. Manhattan fire escapes and suburban backyards were chockablock with eatables, growing where none had ever been seen before. Plants range from the challenging, such as broccoli and eggplant, to the relatively easy to handle garden staples, mint and basil.

A Google search of "recipes with basil" produced 1.2 million results. It also directed me to the more pressing issue: "What to do with too much basil." The pandemic crop I coveted most was tomatoes. My wife, Amy, watched me nurse three tomato plants and determined that I was producing the exotic "nine-dollar variety"—a tomato whose amortized unit cost far exceeds anything you'd pay at a supermarket.

Amazon brought me daily deliveries of potting soil, compost and mulch—most of it in bags triple the size I require, at double the price I would pay at Home Depot. I purchased vermiculite, perlite, steer manure, neem oil and worm castings, along with various potions designed to encourage blossoms to produce fruit.

I watched hours of YouTube videos about growing tomatoes. Most, designed to be inspiring, were downright depressing. The hosts casually displayed row after row of pristine specimens that "you, too, can grow." Except I couldn't. Maybe it's because I used a 4-10-5 fertilizer instead of 6-8-3. Perhaps it's because I didn't invest in a fully-automated drip irrigation system. Or maybe it was just that I don't live in San Diego or Yuma, where the sun always shines.

I've heard that "watching grass grow" is the most tedious horticultural activity. Actually, watching tomatoes grow—or, in my case, not grow—is worse. I was up before dawn to investigate progress. I checked mid-morning, mid-day, mid-afternoon and mid-evening. I learned: A watched tomato plant never fails to boil a gardener's patience.

In September my pandemic garden finally produced a ripe, albeit lumpy tomato. I photographed it and named it Frankie.

I just couldn't bring myself to eat it.

21 / LAUGHTER THERAPY

"When a tragedy occurs, people often feel the presence of humor is suddenly inappropriate. Their attitude seems to say, 'This is no laughing matter.' But I feel the opposite. I believe that laughing matters—and it's more essential for me in the tough times than ever." —Allen Funt

MY CREW AND I were outside a rundown warehouse in Queens, New York, where we had been standing, pretty much at rigid attention, for over an hour. Finally, a young woman with a walkie-talkie and a clipboard came over to inform us, "They're about to take a break so it won't be much longer. He should be out in a few minutes." She turned around and had to do a fast shuffle-step to avoid smashing into Paul Newman as he rushed by. "Are these the 'Candid Camera' guys?" he asked.

I was 39 at the time, a semi-veteran journalist, yet I felt about 13. I was to interview this icon of the cinema, a man I greatly admired, for a "Candid Camera" anniversary special on CBS. Paul Newman had never worked with my father, nor had he ever been caught in a "Candid Camera" gag; I wasn't even sure to what extent he had ever *watched* our show. I had written five questions on an index card and rehearsed them exhaustively, yet I was nervous, no, nauseous, as Newman came over. He was wearing jeans, a white tee shirt and a thin white sweater, the kind of look that made Paul Newman so cool. If I ever dressed that way people would wonder: Why is he wearing two white tops?

"Okay," he said, "let's do this." I managed to say something like, "Yes, of course." But what I was *trying* to say was: this should really be done indoors; you should be dressed more in keeping with the dignity of our prime-time show, and you're not going to wear those sunglasses are you?

"I'll stand right here," he said politely but firmly.

"May I hold your glasses?" I asked.

"No, I'm fine."

"Can we get a sound check?"

"No, I'm sure it's working."

"Okay. Well, I have a few questions here, and..."

"I think I know what you want."

With that, Newman looked into the camera, his gentle expression seemingly focused on each individual living room in America. "I think that 'Candid Camera' is important," he began, "not just because it's funny and not just because it's original. Let me tell you why. A few years ago John Huston was very ill. He had mentioned something to me years before about 'Candid Camera' being his favorite program. So I called Allen and I said, 'John is sick,' and Allen sent over many, many hours of stuff. And whenever Huston would get in the dumps, he'd run that footage, and it would make him laugh. He said that if he could laugh for half an hour, he could go for four hours without pain. That's what I remember most about 'Candid Camera.'"

I explained we'd need a moment to check the tape.

"I'm sure you've got it," he said over his shoulder as he walked back into the warehouse.

Paul Newman's anecdote was similar to stories I've heard for many years, ever since Dad started the nonprofit Laughter Therapy Foundation. In fact, the charity came about because of anecdotal evidence provided by the editor and writer Norman Cousins in his 1979 book "Anatomy of an Illness." Cousins suffered from an extremely painful condition known as ankylosing spondylitis—painful enough just to spell and pronounce—which basically means that the connective tissue in the spine is disintegrating. Chances of a full recovery: about one in 500.

While doctors worked to help him, Cousins took charge of whatever aspects of his care he could, beginning with controlling pain. He was taking 26 aspirin tablets and 12 phenylbutazone pills *per day*, along with codeine and sleeping pills. He asked my father for "Candid Camera" films and a projector for his hospital room.

"It worked," Cousins wrote. "I made the joyous discovery that 10 minutes of genuine belly laughter had an anesthetic effect and would give me at least two hours of pain free sleep. When the pain-killing effect of the laughter wore off, we would switch on the motion-picture projector again, and, not infrequently, it would lead to another pain-free sleep interval."

Cousins and his doctor began doing blood tests to determine if laughter was actually affecting body chemistry for the better. It was. "I was greatly elated by the discovery that there is a physiologic basis for the ancient theory that laughter is good medicine.

"There was, however, one negative side-effect of the laughter from the standpoint of the hospital. I was disturbing other patients."

Because both scientific and anecdotal evidence support the power of laughter, and since "Candid Camera" style humor works particularly well for such purposes, Dad wanted to do more. He created his Laughter Therapy Foundation, with start-up funding from an unlikely source...

A "Candid Camera" staff member, who was fired after just three weeks back in the mid-1960s—but went on to become a successful stand-up comic and TV host—libeled Dad in her autobiography, claiming that he exposed himself during a staff meeting. After the book was published she admitted it was a lie.

"Rather than suing her, as I'm sure she expected," Dad later wrote, "I arranged to have her donate $25,000 to set up Laughter Therapy. It seemed fitting that the money for this project should come as the result of such a laughable accusation."

The terms of the settlement shielded her identity. However, after her death in 2014 I contacted my lawyer to see if the deal remained in effect. "Can we talk?" I asked him. At the end of the $450 call he said maybe I shouldn't print the name.

LAUGHTER THERAPY, WHICH CONTINUES TODAY, provides specially selected "Candid Camera" videos, at no charge, to critically ill people.

I'm not a doctor (although I've played one on TV). However, during a lifetime of observing people in a wide range of situations, I have my own theories about laughter. I don't believe people can be trained to have a sense of humor—everyone has a bit of it, and some folks are fortunate to have more than others. What we can cultivate is a comedic *outlook*. We can learn to identify humorous aspects of life and that, in turn, provides more opportunity for beneficial laughter.

Any LOL experience that releases endorphins is healthy, regardless of the style of comedy. However, "Candid Camera" seems to be particularly effective because it is rooted in reality. That's where the comedic outlook comes in. A patient in Ontario, Canada wrote to us: "I now try to make conscious efforts to search for new ways to see and live, rather than just following 'standard procedures.' I stop more often to appreciate the wonderful absurdities in life." A woman in West Virginia added, "I'm almost over the deep depression that I had. I viewed each [video] several times, and it started me on the track to look for humor in everyday happenings."

A surprising number of books and articles have been written about the benefits of laughter. In terms of science, I'm fascinated. But those authors who claim they can teach people to laugh more—well, they make me laugh. As Mark Twain once observed, "A sense of humor is one thing no one will admit to not having."

Some people seem willing to laugh at just about *anything*. These people annoy me, which, in turn, makes me laugh at the absurdity of their behavior—giving me a beneficial laugh. See how this works? I used to play amateur baseball against a pitcher who laughed just about every time he threw the ball. It drove me crazy when I faced him, to the point where I suspected he was doing it on purpose to gain a competitive edge. Once I saw the humor in his antics, I *owned* his fastball, as we ballplayers like to say.

I HAVE A FRIEND WHO REPLIES TO MY TEXTS with her own humorless Ha Code. A single "ha" conveys zero joviality. It's basically a put-down. I write: "You really gobbled up that second dessert," and she replies, "ha." A double ha—"haha"—makes it seem as if she's at least mildly amused, but she's not. I write: "There are three Starbucks within seven blocks of my office, and they're all busy all the time." She replies, "haha," but she means,"So what?" When she gets to triples and quads—"Hahahaha"—we're into heavy sarcasm. I write, "Do you think Trump assumes Black Friday is a holiday celebrated by African Americans?" She hits me with a string of ha's reminiscent of the late Jackie Gleason's mocking response to lame jokes: "Har-har-hardy-har-har!"

"Haha" and its keyboard counterparts are harmless tools but shouldn't be mistaken as substitutes for actual laughter. Ha Code is as empty of humor as "LOL"—which is the last thing you would say or write if, by chance, you actually found yourself laughing out loud. And what about ":)"? That's a sign of laughter, or at least a smile, right? Not really. It functions as a plea for sympathetic understanding of what might be an overly harsh communiqué. It's most often used by the sender, not the recipient, as in: "Your dress reminded me of our dining room curtains. :)"

Genuine laughter can't really be written out, just as you can't spell the sound of a sneeze, which is why writers settle for "ah-choo." You could try "ah, ha," but that's an announcement of discovery, best delivered emphatically: "Ah, ha!" There's a sly dramatic laugh usually written, "heh, heh, heh," but it fell from favor long before texting was invented.

When I told a friend of my concern about our dependence on symbols masquerading as laughter, he asked, "Then what should one write to convey sincere amusement via text?"

Ah, ha! That depends on whether you're actually laughing or merely acknowledging the sender's attempt at humor. The latter is polite; the former is cathartic, and there is no appropriate symbol for it.

Is our current lifestyle slowly sapping our sense of humor? Or at least our likelihood of having a hearty, endorphin-releasing belly laugh? I picture sad souls typing "hahaha" or "LOL" while sitting alone in office cubicles, or in dreary dorm rooms or surrounded by solemn strangers on the subway.

Life comes with its own laugh track. All you have to do is tap into it rather than type into it.

Laughter is contagious, which is why smart promoters hire a few good laughers to sit in the audience to get things rolling. It's why TV producers use laugh tracks—"sweetening," as it's known—signaling viewers to stop texting long enough to laugh. I don't have research to back me up, but I'm convinced that the millions of people now streaming movies at home are laughing a lot less than folks in theaters.

Oddly, TV executives, the people networks rely upon to pick the best comedy shows, are almost universally incapable of laughing out loud. Often I'd sit in a room with them as they screened what I believed to be my funniest material, and they would not so much as grin. I took it personally until I came to understand that it's a quirk of the profession. The best you'll get from a TV exec when the lights come up is a vacant expression, an almost-imperceptible elevating of one eyebrow, and the words, delivered in a monotone, "That's funny. That's really funny."

Are we all becoming TV execs? :(

◆ ◆ ◆

I wondered if they ever had a "Fire Sale" at a fire department.
The Dallas FD let me do it and even gave us burned stuff to sell.

I LOOK AT LIFE'S EVERYDAY CURIOSITIES and frustrations as potential gags for "Candid Camera."

The word *convenience*, for example. When Ticketmaster adds $15 to my order it's robbery, but the fact that they call it a "Convenience Fee" is really funny. We started adding the word to patter in our gags. "We're from public works and we're installing a fire hydrant in the middle of your front lawn...for your convenience." "I'm with the sanitation department. We're replacing your three recycling bins with *eight* bins...for your convenience."

The zeitgeist is my playbook.

That "clearance bar" at the drive-thru. What if we made it really low? Say, three feet off the ground?

Don't like tipping? How about we place a jar on the counter at a medical office labeled: "Tips for the Doctor appreciated."

Curious about hybrid foods like the "pluot" (plum and apricot)? Why don't we super-glue strawberries on asparagus stalks and market them as *asparaberries?*

Tired of health foods? Sample one of our *Cholester-Rolls*—snacks made entirely from "100% pure cholesterol." (We used tofu.)

Challenged by recycling rules? Our mandatory class for apartment residents teaches how to separate garbage according to color and smell.

Bugged by expiration dates on products? We're selling *clothing* with an expiration date: Don't wear after this date because the garment will be out of style.

Hate door-to-door solicitors? Our actress is at your door selling handy "No Soliciting" signs.

Annoyed by having to show ID? Our store clerk requires *three* types of photo ID...and "something with your thumb print on it."

Gas prices too high? We'll stop your pump mid-fill while we raise the price.

Restroom hand dryers don't work well? Ours is really bad: It blows a fine mist of water.

Dislike banks that chain pens to the counter? You'll love our restaurant that chains silverware to the tables.

Worried about the dry cleaner damaging clothes? Our shop will happily sell you dry cleaning insurance.

Bothered by putting things together Ikea-style? We'll deliver that refrigerator you ordered in 48 pieces with, yes, "some assembly required."

Riled by TSA procedures? We'll instruct air travelers to jump on the conveyor belt and go through the X-ray machine! (On second thought, maybe we skip that gag.)

◆ ◆ ◆

DURING THE YEARS I LIVED IN MANHATTAN I got used to sleeping through screeching sirens, revving engines and even, sadly, the occasional cry for help. In Pebble Beach, things are so quiet that a falling pine cone can be jarring.

Which brings me to the stormy night, just after 3 a.m., when I twisted and turned for 20 painful minutes, wondering why someone in the neighborhood would be blowing a car horn, nonstop.

With Amy fretting and our Shih Tzu Dorothy yapping, I stepped outside to investigate. In the driveway, in pounding rain, my son's 20-year-old Pontiac Grand Am was honking at a volume that would have been annoying in mid-afternoon, but in the dead of night was positively deafening.

Danny was in New York, having left his car in my care. When I got in, my feet plunged into several inches of water. The engine wouldn't start—no surprise there. Yet the horn blared on, seemingly louder than before, which was confounding.

Realizing I had neither the knowledge nor nerve to fiddle with wet wires under the hood, I decided the only course was to drain the battery— hopefully before the police showed up.

I turned on the headlights, defroster, windshield wipers and radio, which happened to be playing "Lady Marmalade," the 1974 tune by Patti LaBelle. My mind ran to volume. Would the battery drain faster if the volume were turned way up?

I had wiper blades scraping, cold air pouring from the defroster, incessant honking, and "Voulez-vous coucher avec moi, ce soir?" at max volume.

Desperate to find humor in this nightmare, my mind ran to semantics. If I were to phone Triple A would I say that my car's horn was stuck because the vehicle was "leaking"? That didn't seem right. When a car leaks oil, for example, the stuff spills out. When a pipe under your sink leaks, water drips onto the floor. But does the word "leak" apply when water collects inside a car?

If not leak, then what? "My car is *absorbing* water"? "*Retaining* water"?

In my delirium I also puzzled over what to call the thing you push to blow the horn. It's not a button or switch. What is that soft area in the center of the steering wheel? The honker? Could this be the only part of a car without a name?

SOME PEOPLE GO THROUGH AN EXPERIENCE like that without cracking a smile.

Not me. I found it rather amusing.

AFTERWORD

A THIRTY-SOMETHING WOMAN was pouring my refill at a coffee shop in Florida and gushed, "You're the most famous person I've ever met."

Feeling ashamed that I wasn't Brad Pitt, I tripled her tip and headed for the parking lot.

Back in California the following week, I set up a "Candid Camera" gag to examine fame . . .

Three of our people pretended to be from a local TV station. With their camera and audio equipment in full view, they approached a random person for a quick man-on-the-street interview, something about "high interest rates." This scene was secretly photographed by the real "Candid Camera" team in a van across the street. As soon as the news crew finished, our actress approached the interviewee and asked for an autograph: "I just saw you being interviewed, you're famous!" It was fascinating because some folks became embarrassed and tried to deflect the autograph seeker, while others were swept up in the adoration and happily signed. We sent over another person: "I just saw you signing an autograph. Are you famous?" Soon, a small crowd formed in a scene that I imagine Andy Warhol would have appreciated as proof that everyone has "15 minutes of fame."

ON AN AUGUST EVENING in 2018 I made my entrance at the Reg Lenna Theater in Jamestown, New York, and looked out at 191 smiling faces in a space built to accommodate over a thousand. At that same moment Amy Schumer was doing her comedy act a few blocks away in a sold-out hockey arena. Taken aback by the size of our audience, I announced: "As you can see we've set-up a big video screen tonight and I've arranged for a live feed of Amy Schumer's show." They found the crack to be very funny, which made me feel marginally better.

While in Jamestown I visited the Lucille Ball Desi Arnaz Museum, honoring the First Lady of television comedy, who was born in Jamestown in 1911. Later, I took in a one-woman cabaret style show featuring Lucy's daughter, Lucie Arnaz. Lucie began performing professionally when she was 15 (I made my first network TV appearance at 16). She followed closely in her mother's footsteps on "The Lucy Show" and then for six seasons as a regular on "Here's Lucy." Lucie managed to craft her own successful career in TV, film and stage. She made her Broadway debut in the 1979 musical "They're Play-ing Our Song," and has won numerous awards for acting and singing, while zigging and zagging through show business in search of her own identity.

Lucie told me she felt her path had been "a blessing and somewhat of a curse." She was quick to add, "as with any curse, you must be stronger than that. I know what I do is valuable. I know I have been trained well. I have had a pretty consistent, profitable career in this business. But, after 50 years doing what I do, if I am not working at something specific, in people's minds I simply revert to the default position: 'Lucille Ball's Daughter.' I've had to make my peace with the fact that this will never change and I must, simply, embrace it and not absorb it as if it were an insult."

When I watch Lucie perform I marvel at how talented she is. She exists in so much reflected glory, yet shines so brightly on her own.

"I loved my folks and no one did what they did better," she stressed. "I am fortunate to have been born into their galaxy. If I stay in gratitude, I am just fine."

Back at the hotel in Jamestown I encountered a guy at the lobby bar who had seen a poster for our stage show. He knew the name Funt, and had watched "Candid Camera," but something, maybe it was the gray hair, left him confused. He smiled and said:

"Do you know who you used to be?"

OUTDEX

Certain readers (I'm looking at you, Mayim) start with the Index to see if they're mentioned. What I'm offering is a handy Outdex of people who are *not* mentioned in this book.

Berlin, Irving: I was shooting a "Candid Camera" holiday special and the gag was to have a strolling violinist who could only play one song. I picked "White Christmas." We shot for five hours and got great stuff, and then our office suggested I had better clear it with the composer. I called the great Mr. Berlin, who was 101 at the time, and he said, "absolutely positively not!" (I had to toss the footage and start over with "Jingle Bells.")

Burnett, Carol: When I visited her in Santa Barbara in 2019 she regaled me with stories about working with Dad on Garry Moore's variety show. Her favorite (and mine): Asking guys to carry her suitcase to the corner because "I've been lugging it for ten blocks." They couldn't budge it. (The suitcase contained 200 pounds of bricks.)

Buttigieg, Pete: I covered him at close range during his presidential campaign. He was the only candidate who never once stumbled with a reporter's question. (Wears inexpensive clothes but really fancy watches.)

Carson, Johnny: Early in his career Johnny auditioned to be the co-host on "Candid Camera." My father told him, "You're a personable young man, but you'll never make it on television." (For decades after that, Dad could only appear on "The Tonight Show" on Mondays—when Johnny was off.)

Clinton, Bill: While president he played a round of golf at Pebble Beach at dawn. I followed along, discovering that he had the Trumpian habit of reloading when he didn't like his original shot. (Also: The Secret Service carried high-powered rifles in golf bags.)

Fingers, Rollie: I played for a few years on what was known as the Celebrity Players Golf Tour. My first partner was the Hall of Fame pitcher with the big handlebar mustache and scowl that frightened Big League hitters. Scared to death, I flubbed my first shot, then turned to see Rollie smash his own club into the ground in disgust. (I never got over it, and the other guys still haven't stopped laughing about it.)

Flagg, Fannie: Never a co-host, but hands down the First Lady of "Candid Camera," doing over 100 gags with Dad and me. My fave: Fannie is a customer at a drive-in bank—and plows her sports car right through the wall. (Tellers were gobsmacked.)

Ford, Gerald: Not long after his presidency, he spoke at a business retreat that I attended. Several of us got seriously drunk, stood quite near him, and laughed throughout his entire talk. We could have been arrested. (Although I imagine Ford would have pardoned us.)

Hitchcock, Alfred: My pal Steve Zuckerman and I were crossing the street near Grand Central Station in 1976 when we spotted the famous film director. (Ever seen photos of the guy? You couldn't *not* spot him in public.) After first denying who he was he drew for each of us a perfect profile, the one used as the logo on his TV shows. (Coolest autograph I've ever seen.)

Hewitt, Don: Crown publishing hired me to write a book about Hewitt's secret techniques as boss of "60 Minutes." When he learned I was poking around he hit the roof and managed to kill my project. He actually sent me a threatening letter that said, "Does your father know what you're doing?" (Short answer: yes and he was quite proud.)

Letterman, David: Dave wanted to run our Richard Lewis footage (see Chapter 15). He assured his staff he could jump on the phone with me and get me to grant permission. I said no, which explains why I never appeared on the Letterman show. (Sorry, Dave. I was a total jerk.)

Nixon, Richard: The guy in the ill-fitting tan raincoat, waiting to mail a letter at a Manhattan post office, was the disgraced former president, the year after he resigned. He told me he was filing his tax return and always preferred to mail it himself—though he didn't say whether he had cheated. (I noticed that black hairs were growing on the bridge of his rather large nose.)

Owens, Terrell: When he was with the 49ers I caught him in a gag by pretending to be a sports reporter doing a live radio interview. Understandably, T.O. wanted to talk about himself, and I only asked questions about the team's rookies. After my ninth straight question on that topic, he said, "Who cares about rookies? I don't!" (What a character.)

Parton, Dolly: A fictional Dolly is mentioned in Chapter 15, but the *real* Dolly did gags on "Candid Camera" back in the 1970s. In one bit she pretended to have an injured ankle and persuaded men to carry her to her car. The parking lot had a dozen cars that all looked like the one she described (and, "she's an armful, if you know Dolly," Dad quipped to viewers). In 2021 I offered Dolly the job as my new co-host on "Candid Camera," but she "passed" (which is an industry term meaning, "why would I want to do that?").

Philbin, Regis: Like Dolly Parton, I mentioned Regis only tangentially. I went on his show a half-dozen times to plug "Candid Camera," and each time he asked, "Can you do a gag with our audience?" Nobody rebuffed Regis. So I tried the bits, which were always bad because you can't do our hidden-camera work with an audience in a TV studio. (It didn't really matter, because even with a bad gag, Regis was never not entertaining.)

Quinn, Martha: I was fortunate that the first promotable female I ever worked with on national TV was Martha, at the height of her popularity as an original "VJ" on MTV. We were doing a cable-TV awards show. (Simply put, she was great and I was awful.)

Seinfeld, Jerry: Due respect to Jerry and Larry David, "Candid Camera" is the original show about *nothing*. Jerry not only borrowed our nothingness, he also took up residence in our family's former apartment on 81st Street in Manhattan. (Note to Jerry: Cameras are hidden above each fireplace, and there are two in the master bedroom.)

Van Dyke, Dick: In 2012, just before his 87th birthday, Dick appeared with me at a fundraiser for a hospital in Santa Cruz, California. My job was to interview him on stage for an hour. One of the best tributes you can pay a performer is that he's every bit as nice off-screen as on. That's Dick. "I can still trip over that ottoman," he told me, referring to the opening of "The Dick Van Dyke Show." "Only now it really hurts." (A true legend.)

Winfrey, Oprah: I was a guest on her program twice, at the fortress-like studio she built in Chicago. Among the guests the second time around was the actress Shirley Jones, who, like me, was asked to sign a performers' agreement. I thought nothing of it until two days later when I read in the trade papers that Jones and her husband Marty Ingels had filed a complaint against Oprah. Apparently, despite her enormous wealth, she was squeezing her guests out of proper union wages. Also: The day before the show Oprah's people asked me if they could do their own hidden-camera gag and run it before I came on. I said, "No, I'm showing several of my clips, so please don't." They said ok. As I stood in the wings, Oprah said, "Before we bring out Peter, I want to show you a joke we pulled on our audience before the show, using our hidden cameras!" (I tried to be cool, but the more I think about it the least Oprah could have done was give me . . . a new car!)

ACKNOWLEDGEMENTS

I'm lucky to be surrounded by smart people. Not necessarily funny, but definitely smart. My wife Amy, daughter Stephanie and son Danny (pictured below) head that list. Thanks to their collective judgment I had to do more rewrites than planned.

My brothers, John and Bill, and sisters, Patricia and Juliet, have always been supportive. As the oldest, I've sometimes felt like a surrogate for our Dad, an impossible task. Allen Funt was unique, and we miss him very much.

My friend since we worked at ABC News, Clarence Fanto, is a sharp-eyed editor. Mike Shatzkin, with whom I grew up in Croton, is a publishing guru. Together, they tried to keep me on track. Producer Brian Courrejou at the "Candid Camera" office has an uncanny ability to remember things about my past that I've managed to forget.

I would also like to acknowledge the inspiration provided by my second grade teacher Mrs. Corwin, who wrote on my report card: "Peter is extremely average."

FREE VIDEO DOWNLOAD

As a bonus for reading to the final page, please enjoy a free video download of 15 full-length "Candid Camera" sequences discussed in Self-Amused. Here's what you get in over an hour of smiles:

Peter Plays a Roman Statue (page 24)
Jamestown Baseball Pitcher (page 49)
N.Y. Yankees Gag (page 53)
Restaurant Reservations (page 84)
Beaut-o-Matic (page 130)
Suzanne's Smell-Free Perfume (page 138)
Dina Tickets Folks in Driveways (page 143)
Richard Lewis, 2 clips (page 149)
A Date for Donald Trump (page 159)
CBS Birthday Cake (page 160)
TV Critics & Mister Rogers (page 166)
Dirty Words (page 175)
Airport Security (page 177)
Restaurant Face Masks (page 193)
NYC Trash Bins (page 207)

To obtain your free video, for viewing online or to download, send an email to: Amused@CandidCamera.com. Include proof of your book purchase—or just state where and when the purchase was made and the price paid. You will be emailed a unique code for use at Vimeo. (You may also direct questions and comments to the same email address.)